# faith

When Bill decided to leave the USA and move to Russia, our family was crushed. It was like a death for us and we thought he had gone insane and that we would probably never see him again. When he left his medical practice, he had arranged everything so carefully that there was no turning back for him. He sold or gave away everything he owned. We cried often and our family talked about it for years. It felt like he had died. Only now, more than 20 years later do we understand and rejoice as we see the *Hand of God* in Bill's decision to follow God. It was impossible for our family to understand when it happened. Only God could see the future from Bill's obedience, and what God did with it is truly amazing. But, after all, we do serve an amazing miracle working God, if we have *faith*.

—**Dough and Nancy Hopkins**, Brother-in-law and sister

For over 25 years it has been my joy and privilege to help people share their faith stories on national television as co-host of *100 Huntley Street,* Canada's longest running daily talk show. Dr. Bill Becknell is one of my favorites! The Chief of Surgery at his local hospital in Kentucky was in a place of brokenness when God reminded him of a promise he made years earlier in a life-threatening crisis. He owned 5 Kentucky farms, 250 head of Registered Angus Cattle, a Jaguar, a Cadillac, a pickup truck, and his own airplane. In 1993 he sold it all to share the love of God with unreached people in Russia through medical evangelism. Dr. Becknell soon drove a new vehicle. I think of him as a true Santa who often delivers medical kits by reindeer-drawn sleigh to people who live above the Arctic Circle!

Agape Medical Center, Agape Farm, Agape Guesthouse, Orphan Half Way House, Home for Unwed Mothers, church plants and Russian

Hallelulia (an interdenominational gathering for fellowship and worship imported from Kentucky)—no wonder today it is Agape *Unlimited-Russia*! What a thrill to have this story so beautifully told and with pictures—a portrait of the Apostle Paul's encouragement:

*"Everything that we have—right thinking and right living, a clean slate and a fresh start—comes from God by way of Jesus Christ"* (1 Corinthians 1:28, The Message).

—**Moira Brown**, Co-host of 100 Huntley Street, Crossroads Christian Communications, Inc., Canada

Dr. Bill Becknell is one of my heroes in the faith.

As a 14-year old boy, "Dr. Bill" promised God he'd go to the "ends of the earth" with the Gospel. Thirty-five years later, he kept that promise when he left a successful surgical practice in Manchester, Kentucky. He sold or gave away all of his possessions, his cattle farms, his fancy car, and private plane. He packed all he owned into 13 boxes and flew to Russia, even though he didn't know a single Russian and couldn't speak the language. There he founded Agape Unlimited—Russia, and began medical outreaches to villages above the Arctic Circle.

Dr. Bill travels by snowmobile, reindeer sleigh, truck and helicopter to reach people who have never seen a doctor or heard about Jesus. Shepherds have told him that they've been waiting all their lives for someone to explain to them about the "god" who made the stars they see at night.

Every trip is a story. He reaches prisoners who cut holes in the ice so they can be baptized, shepherds who have never seen a Bible, and Nenets (Eskimos) who travel across the tundra in search of pasture for their reindeer herds.

He never talks of slowing down—only what still needs to be done.

Dr. Bill founded Russia's first Christian health clinic that reaches more than 10,000 patients a year. When Agape acquired a farm in 2011, it didn't take long for him to envision a place for children aging out of orphanages, a guest house on the farm for children facing surgery or chemotherapy in Moscow, and a home for pregnant moms who want to keep their babies.

His story is packed with adventure and intrigue, but most of all it's packed with radical faith in our great God.

—**Ruth Schenk**, Correspondent/Staff Writer
Southeast Christian Church Outlook, Louisville, KY

From 1993, Dr. Bill Becknell has devoted his life to Russia. A surgeon, Dr. Bill gave up his practice in the U.S. to serve Christ in Russia. It was a privilege for my late husband, Peter, and me to meet Dr. Bill soon after he arrived in Moscow and began the AGAPE ministry. How greatly God has blessed Dr. Bill's faithfulness over the past 21 years. AGAPE has sponsored hundreds of mobile medical expeditions across Russia. Since 2005, the Agape Clinic, which Dr. Bill founded, has cared for 429,563 patients. AGAPE has helped provide education for many Russian health care professionals. In 2011, Dr. Bill started the Agape Farm near Moscow, where hundreds of children attend Bible camps and other gospel outreach is happening. *FAITH* recounts not only the amazing ways God has used Agape, but reveals the power of one life, committed to Christ and His kingdom.

—**Dr. Anita Deyneka**, Co-founder of Russian Ministries
and director of A Home for Every Orphan

I have been privileged to know Dr. Bill Becknell (or Dr. Bill as our family calls him) for over 20 years. From the early days of his ministry in Russia, he would come to Helsinki, Finland, where we lived for medical supplies. Dr. Bill's story is unique, exciting and shows how God takes to heart the promises we give Him—and how God keeps His promises to guide, protect, and to bless us in our obedience to Him—even to the "Top of the Earth."

Dr. Bill's story is riveting, entertaining—and true. It could be fiction except that it is true! The reader will travel alongside Dr. Bill as he traverses the frozen wastelands of the high Russian Arctic in a reindeer sleigh and be with him as he ministers to the people living in these remote places. A unique and exciting read!

—**Ari Uotila**, World Vision Canada

My father and I have always been close. Even though he was a busy dad studying for medical school when I was young, he always made time to do things with me. We would look at things together under his microscope he used in his studies, played with Hot Wheels cars and had race tracks set up all over the living room (I was never much of one for dolls!) and climb up on the garage roof to look at the stars at nights. Even when he was busy studying, I would sit at his large study table with him and make things with paper, scissors and tape like party hats for my white pet rat Squeaky he snuck home from the lab for me.

After going through a series of tragedies and a very difficult time in his life, Dad announced he felt the Lord calling him into missions and particularly to Russia. Most family and friends thought he had flipped his lid. I knew my Dad had a very close and personal relationship with the Lord and I was not all that surprised by his calling and knew he was willing to go and do whatever the Lord asked of him. The hard part was knowing how much we would miss him and how very far away he would be! I was married by this time and we had a son, Trevor, who was only 2 years old when his Grandpa left to go to "the ends of the earth" to take the gospel to those who had never heard the name of Jesus and of his saving grace and love for them. He sold everything he had and went to a country halfway around the world where he knew no one and couldn't even speak the language and trusted God to show him the way—what faith!

It was hard not being able to pick up the phone and call or see him on special family occasions, but I always knew he was where God wanted him and even though we missed him terribly, he was doing the work God had laid before him and he was making a difference in people's lives for eternity. Today, Trevor loves his Grandpa dearly, and even though they don't get to spend as much as time together as they would like, they are very close. Today we are very grateful for the improvements in technology which allow us to be able to talk by phone and internet much more easily (and cheaper!) today than when he first went 20+ years ago!

I will never forget the very first pictures Dad sent to us from one of his medical mission trips up above the Arctic Circle with the Nenets people. They lived in animal skin teepees out on the tundra and herded reindeer. Before he left, my husband Louis and I would tease Dad about being so cold natured—he would come to visit and, even though it was 70 degrees outside, he would have on a T-shirt, long-sleeve denim shirt and his leather "bomber" jacket and would still be cold. So the first time he sent those pictures from above the Arctic Circle, I thought, "This cannot be my Dad!" But, along with taking care of all the other details, God even adjusted his internal thermostat and somehow he survived! How we have enjoyed his tales of all the miracles and many ways God has led and provided for him along his journey of faith! So thankful for God's love and provision for him! Now, some 20+ years later, it is so amazing to look back and see what God has done and how many lives have been touched for eternity through the obedience and love of one man and I am very proud and blessed to call him my father.

—**Shawn Tucker**, Daughter

At the ICMDA conference for Christian doctors in Norway 1994, we met a colleague with a vision to reach minority people in Russia. He was giving them healthcare and the Love of God. We got to know a man with a conviction to go on God's call. During twenty years, we saw more and more of Dr. Bill Becknell´s visions come true. In all the different situations, Bill asks God for the right way to go. His amazing book is about the "faith" to follow God to the "Ends of the Earth." This book is an encouragement for all Christians.

Through the years we have met Bill both in Sweden and Russia. The results of Bill´s work really impress us.

—**Dr. Rune** and **Kerstin Björke'**, Borlänge Sweden
**Dr. Göran** and **Gudrun Klemetz**, Falun Sweden
**Lars-Åke** and **Elisabeth Lundquist**, Stockholm Sweden

I met Dr. Bill Becknell in 1995 at the International Christian Chamber of Commerce in Sweden where he was a speaker. After listening to him talk about the Agape ministry in Russia, I decided to participate in an expedition. After that expedition Agape, Germany was formed as a German partner to support the work in Russia. It has been an amazing adventure to see all that God has done through Bill.

From my point of view, Bill is a really brave soldier. His life was, is and will always be a battle for the Lord. This book is about his battles of "faith" and will be an encouragement to everyone who reads it.

—**Ingeborg Fuhrhop-Stetzler**, President, Agape Germany

# faith

THE ABYSS WE ALL FACE

# Dr. Bill Becknell

NEW YORK

# fa*i*th
## THE ABYSS WE ALL FACE

Published in New York, New York, by Morgan James Publishing. Morgan James and The Entrepreneurial Publisher are trademarks of Morgan James, LLC. www.MorganJamesPublishing.com

The Morgan James Speakers Group can bring authors to your live event. For more information or to book an event visit The Morgan James Speakers Group at www.TheMorganJamesSpeakersGroup.com.

A **free** eBook edition is available with the purchase of this print book.

ISBN 978-1-63047-416-4  paperback
ISBN 978-1-63047-417-1  eBook
ISBN 978-1-63047-418-8  hardcover
Library of Congress Control Number: 2014949389

CLEARLY PRINT YOUR NAME ABOVE IN UPPER CASE

**Instructions to claim your free eBook edition:**
1. Download the BitLit app for Android or iOS
2. Write your name in **UPPER CASE** on the line
3. Use the BitLit app to submit a photo
4. Download your eBook to any device

**Cover Design by:**
Rachel Lopez
www.r2cdesign.com

**Interior Design by:**
Bonnie Bushman
bonnie@caboodlegraphics.com

In an effort to support local communities, raise awareness and funds, Morgan James Publishing donates a percentage of all book sales for the life of each book to Habitat for Humanity Peninsula and Greater Williamsburg.

Get involved today, visit
www.MorganJamesBuilds.com

**Habitat for Humanity**
Peninsula and
Greater Williamsburg
Building Partner

There is no greater "**<u>JOY</u>**" than
following Jesus even if He leads you
to the "Ends of the Earth."
I know, I have been there and back!
W. E. Becknell Jr. M.D.

# dedication

This book is dedicated to my best friend.
Jesus Christ.

# table of contents

# foreword

I first met Dr. Becknell, or Dr. Bill as he is affectionately known, in November 2001 while attending a Focus on the Family medical conference with my wife. At the time, I was feeling our Lord's leading to be involved in Christian medical missions, and thought I could find some service opportunities at the conference. Like most people when thinking of medical missions, I thought of Africa or South America, and certainly some place warm and tropical. Growing up and living in West Texas, the last place I would have considered would have been Siberia! Still, after spending a little time with Dr. Bill, it was hard not to be infected by his love of our Lord, and by his faith. Mustering my courage, I joined Dr. Bill in 2002 for an expedition and I can honestly say my life has never been the same since! It has now been my pleasure to minister beside Dr. Bill for the past 13 years!

As you read "Faith, The Abyss We All Face" my hope is that you will not only enjoy a good story about one man's journey, but also come away with a deeper understanding concerning faith. What is faith? Is faith simply belief or is it something more? What is the purpose of faith? What is the inter-relationship between faith and works? By telling his personal story and taking you along on his journey, these are some of the deeper questions that Dr. Bill answers. Enjoy the journey as he takes you from growing up in the woods of Appalachia and going with his father, a family physician, as he makes house calls deep in the mountains, to returning to Appalachia later in life as a successful surgeon. Continue the journey as he travels through personal brokenness, remembers a promise to God and serves in Somalia as a medical missionary, and finally surrenders to God, which ultimately leads to serving in Russia. Throughout the journey, I think you will come away with a sense of God's presence, despite life's circumstances, and the Joy that can be found through living a life of faith and "following Jesus, even if He leads you to the "Ends of the Earth"!

—**David DeShan**, M.D.
President
Agape Unlimited, Inc.

# acknowledgements

This book would have been written in "hillbilleze" if it were not for two very special and talented people. People who taught me more English than I ever learned in school. The school was not at fault. I just loved science, biology and dissecting frogs more than English and Shakespeare.

I had two wonderful editors. They were great. It was a joy to work with them and at times it was a lot of fun. I write like I talk, but for some strange reason that doesn't work well when you are trying to publish a book… or so they tell me.

When I say "it was cold". I really wanted to say… "IT WAS ***REALLY*** COLD!!!!!!" So, we were constantly quarreling about how to put the "emotion" into printed words. I learned a lot.

I still think my way of expressing emotions is better than what the literary world allows, but when publishing a book, you have to obey the publisher's guidelines. Which we did……… most, … of the time. (Did you notice that there were more than (3 dots) … after the word did?

And a comma that doesn't belong there either… but the pause works nice in speech.

My sincere heartfelt thanks and appreciations goes out to two very wonderful ladies who "never gave up" on helping me put this story into print.

Pat Mohney lives in Moscow and has worked with Agape for many years. What a blessing to have such a dependable and faithful servant nearby. She also helps to write our Agape E-Flashes, as well as her own stories and blogs about her life in Russia. She has learned to laugh and not cry at my craziness, which helps to keep her healthy. **Pro 17:22**—A joyful heart is good medicine…

Nancy Toback who is of Italian descent was fun to work with. She taught me a lot about editing. Sadly, I teased her a lot because she is a city "gal" from NYC, now living in sunny Florida and hates cold weather. And yet, somehow a miracle happened and God touched her heart to sign up for an Agape expedition to one of those "End of the Earth" places in Russia. She trusted God and stepped into that "abyss" of faith, completely out of her comfort zone, and learned that God was there to hold her safe and secure in His arms. And amazingly, she also learned how to open a farm gate!

My sincere thanks goes to Pat Mohney and Nancy Toback for their wonderful and amazing help.

—**W. E. Becknell Jr MD**

# Introduction

This book is about "faith" and the
journey of one person along that road.

It was written to encourage all believers young and old in their
walk of faith. Non-believers may also find the stories and adventures
interesting to read and apply to their lives, because "faith" is something
everyone has.

It is my story of a journey to the literal "Ends of the Earth."
And, what I found there was unexpected…
<< JOY >>
There were extreme hardships, sacrifices, miracles and some near-death
experiences, but the unexpected surprise was the JOY that came from
following Jesus.
"There is no greater JOY than following Jesus…
Even if He leads you to the Ends of the Earth."
I know…
I have been there and returned!
This is my story about what God can do when we listen and obey.

# lost on the tundra!

f aith...

All religions have it ... even Atheists have it!

We all have it. But, what is it?

It is fundamental for Christians, Jews, Muslims, Hindus, Buddhists, and yes, even Atheists. Everyone has "faith." Even if you are psychotic, you have faith in the irrational and fantasy thoughts you have.

What is faith? Why do we need faith? What good is it? Who cares anyway?

Faith affects our lives, every day, in many ways. When the crusaders killed thousands of people in the name of "God," they acted in faith. When a psychotic picks up a gun and kills scores of people, or a terrorist screams out the name of his "god" and plunges the aircraft to earth killing everyone on board, they all have "faith" in what they are doing.

It is important to remember that another person's faith not only affects them…but "us" too!

Faith is essential in our morals, ethics, and in every aspect of our life. We have faith in our spouse, our children, government, banks, schools, even our cars, whether they will start when we turn the key. When Atheists say they don't believe in God, they also have "faith." Their faith is in "themselves," in what "they think" is true. It is the same for everyone.

But the thoughts we think are not "faith."

Your "faith" can also change. Once you believed that something or someone was "true," but then you discovered that it or they were "false." The people of the Soviet Union were devastated by the loss of their country. Everything they had "believed in" was suddenly … gone. Our faith can change over time.

I don't believe that you can have a "faith" that doesn't move. It is either getting bigger, or smaller, never staying the same. As soon as you stop advancing in your faith, you have already started in a backward direction. Faith does not "stagnate" but is always moving. Either forward or backward.

We try to convince others that our "faith" is the correct one. But, if people cannot "see" our faith in the things we do, most likely they will not believe us when we talk about it.

This book is an attempt to "describe" faith as it has affected my life, changed my thoughts, and ultimately my behavior. Some people feel that my story is interesting, and that it may encourage others in their "faith." So, this book is being written more for their benefit, not mine.

I will receive little or no financial gain from this book. I do not seek any fame or fortune from this project. It was a lot of hard work, but if it will encourage others on their journey of faith, then it will have been worth the effort.

I was born and raised in the Appalachian Mountains, but now I have lived continuously inside Russia for more than 20 years. It is my new home. How did I get here? How could I leave my USA home, family, and medical practice to come here? Faith is the essential part of that story.

My faith and my history are rooted in Christianity. But the principals of faith are the same whether you are Jewish, Muslim, Hindu, Buddhist ... or Atheist.

Faith affects everyone's life as well as those around us. I hope this book will help to open a window in your life for others to see how faith has touched your life and changed it for the benefit of you and others around you. Our faith always affects others as well as ourselves.

Oswald Chambers wrote in his book, *My Utmost for His Highest*, that God works through the circumstances of our lives.

> *The circumstances of a saint's life are ordained of God. In the life of a saint there is no such thing as chance. God by His providence brings you into circumstances that you can't understand at all, but the Spirit of God understands. God brings you to places, among people, and into certain conditions to accomplish a definite purpose through the intercession of the Spirit in you.[1]*

---

1   Taken from *My Utmost for His Highest* by Oswald Chambers (November 7), edited by James Reimann, © 1992 by Oswald Chambers Publications Assn., Ltd., and used by permission of Discovery House Publishers, Grand Rapids MI 49501. All rights reserved.

Most of my life, I "never believed" what Oswald Chambers wrote about the circumstances in our lives. I was too "logical" and believed too much in "common sense." But as I discovered, common sense and logic are **not** faith.

Now I understand this! I have both seen it and "experienced" it.

Faith is not a "**goal**" we seek, but faith is a "**process**" we go though in order to reach that goal. How we go through that "**process**" to reach the goal will determine the strength of our faith.

I hope these true stories will help you "to not be afraid" to step off into the unknown abyss of faith by believing, trusting, knowing, and having the "faith" that God **will** keep His promises. I have learned that He *always* keeps His promises. Sadly, it is "us" who do not keep our promises to God, or even to each other. We really are the "unprofitable servants" (Luke 17:5-10).

Here is a true statement.

**There is no greater "JOY" than following God, even if He leads you to the "Ends of the Earth."**

I know...

I have been there... and returned to share this amazing journey with you.

Agape

W. E. Becknell Jr M.D

# CHAPTER ONE

# the promise

i t was cold…

I mean…*"**really**"* cold…

It was the middle of winter in Russia, and tonight the temperature was less than -30 C. I had never been in weather this severe in my entire life. We were well above the Arctic Circle on this night… or maybe it was day? I couldn't tell. Because daylight does not exist here from December through January.

Here I was, standing in this frozen desert with my new, heavy-duty Arctic LL Bean goose down coat, and feeling very "out of place." My hood was up, my gloves were on, and I was shaking inside from the cold and the anxiety.

I was standing outside a small frost-covered metal building on the edge of the tundra. Off in the distance was "nothing" but white. I could not even see a horizon. A light misty snow was falling slowly past a lonely streetlight on the edge of the civilized world, and the men inside the building were busy preparing our reindeer sleds.

I had just asked a question and I really wanted to know the answer.

"Why are we leaving at midnight, instead of in the morning?"

Our tundra guide said, "We are leaving at midnight so that the lakes and rivers will be frozen. This way there is less chance that we will fall through the ice."

*Our tundra guide was 100% serious! This was not a joke or some unnecessary comment. Above is a photo I took of a memorial marker to a man who fell through the ice the week before we traveled this way!*

That was not very comforting or what I wanted to hear! I wish I hadn't asked.

Our host handed us some very "stinky" reindeer skins to put on and we climbed onto the sleigh, and suddenly, we were off with a jerk. Our host was waving good-bye to us, and his image quickly faded into the snowy mist. Within a few seconds, his figure was gone.

We were now "racing" across the frozen tundra in the middle of the night on the back of a wooden reindeer sleigh pulled by a Russian snowmobile that was ready to give up and die at any minute. The distant lights of the small settlement could be seen inside the snow cloud that quickly faded behind us. A snowy mist escaped from under the front of the snowmobile to circle around and surround us in an icy cloud of snow spray.

That was "the beginning" of an unforgettable journey to the "Ends of the Earth"… or should I say "The Top of the World"?

As the sleigh flew across the frozen tundra for the next eight hours, and we became lost for several additional hours, I had time to think.

What in the world am I doing here? This is stupid!

How did I get here?

Why am I putting my life and the life of my translator at risk for death? She has two small kids at home. Maybe I should not have asked her to come with me?

Am I crazy? This could be a disaster!

I started to pray…

*Lord, here I am far above the Arctic Circle, traveling on a reindeer sleigh across the tundra in the middle of the night. It is -30 C, and my driver has told me we are traveling at night because we'll have less chance of falling through the ice on the lakes and rivers…!*

*Am I doing what you want?*

*Is this where you want me to be?*

*Please forgive me for all these questions and doubts. I truly believe it was your calling that brought me to Russia, and I am trying my best to obey. But, I am scared for the safety of my translator and me. Did I make the right decision to come here?*

Full of uncertainty and unanswered questions, I was more concerned for my translator than myself. I was living on a borrowed second life, and so it was not a big deal if I died…but my translator is the mother of two small children.

The night ride was so picturesque! There are no words to describe the incredible beauty of that night as it reflected the moonlight with "zillions" of sparkles that surrounded us like diamonds everywhere we looked. It was incredibly beautiful and peaceful.

*Diamonds in the snow near a village in the Far North.*

I started praising and thanking God for each one of those little "sparkles" off the moonlight, and for all the Love He had given me through His Son Jesus Christ. Then with the adrenalin flowing and my heart pounding inside my chest…

I could hear God whisper…

*"Relax…*

*I have you exactly where I want you. You are in the palm of my hand!"*

An amazing peace flooded me, and I knew I was okay. Safe. I was now "one" with my Heavenly Father, and nothing else mattered.

The answer to all those questions about "how I got here" began many years ago with my childhood in the mountains of Eastern Kentucky.

I was flying across the frozen tundra tonight, not knowing where I was going, putting my life and the life of my translator into the hands of a man we had never met before today, because of a "promise." A promise I made to God when I was a teenager, and now, I was here to keep that promise.

My journey to Russia begins with a promise…

## A Day at the Farm

It all began as an ordinary day during my early teenage years…

*Then…*

*Suddenly…there was an explosion of beautiful colors…*

*No noise…*

*No pain…but,*

*Now, I lay paralyzed on the ground.*

*I was in severe pain,*

*I could not breathe.*

*My clothes were on fire and I was seconds away from dying.*

*This is the story of what happened that day, and how it led me to Russia. It changed my life forever!*

It was a hot summer afternoon in Eastern Kentucky, typical of what we call "dog days" of August, but as I remember, this was June. (Some people say the phrase "dog days" comes from the ancient Romans and has something to do with a star named Sirius.)

But, not in Eastern Kentucky. To understand what is meant by "dog days" you must visit the Appalachian Mountains in August and look at the dogs. These usually rambunctious and playful hound dogs normally jump all over you, but in summer they look dead.

They are lying lifeless on the front porch of a house or mobile home that sits among the green trees on the mountainside. But if you look closely, they are breathing…barely. These dogs are lying in the shade with their tongues hanging out, "panting" for their next breath of air.

Each breath looks like their last. If you come near them, they will not even lift their heads, but they might have enough energy to move their eyes and glance up at you. Otherwise, no other body parts are working.

On days like this it is difficult to do anything. Simply moving and breathing is hard work. The humidity is so high you sweat like Niagara Falls, and any movement feels like you are swimming in molasses.

That's why we call 'em "dog days."

The weather is not fit for a dog!

Today was one of those days.

The sun was beating down on me and I was "burning up" as people would say. I was wearing a thin, short-sleeved shirt and it was "wringing wet" with sweat.

My mother was kind enough to drive us from our small town to what we called "the chicken farm" out on Island Creek. My father had a busy medical practice in this part of the world and was loved and respected by all his patients. He was as close to the TV's *Marcus Welby MD* as anyone you would ever meet in real life.

I never met another doctor like him. He loved medicine, and he loved the "art" of medical practice. He loved and cared about his patients, the mountain culture that he called home, and agriculture. The world could use more doctors like him.

Unfortunately, medical practice is a business today, thanks to the government and insurance companies. This "golden age" of medicine in which he practiced is gone. But, I find it really strange that people think putting a huge government organization or large bureaucratic "for-profit" insurance company between the patient and the doctor will result in better and cheaper medical care.

We already know the government cannot even manage a monopoly like the post office, and to think they can do a better job managing medical care at a cheaper cost is absurd.

My father once told me that over one-third of his patients didn't pay their bills. Still, he never refused to help anyone whether they paid their bills or not. They continued to be his patients, and he felt like it was his responsibility to try to help them, no matter who they were or what they owed him.

## Back to the Farm

This was his "chicken farm," because my dad loved not only medicine, but agriculture. He was born and raised in the mountains, and his family lived close to nature in the hills of Eastern Kentucky. Most everything they needed they raised in a garden or on their small hillside farm. As a young boy he plowed the family farm with a team of mules, and because he was the oldest, it was his responsibility to take care of the family. His father had a job that required a lot of travel, so he was not home much to help with the farm chores.

Dad had planned to graduate from the College of Agriculture at a mountain college, but in his last year he decided to pursue his dream of being a doctor and applied for medical school at the University of Louisville.

He had written the U of L Medical School many letters when he was a child, asking how to apply to medical school. He applied and was accepted with his first application. He used to say it was only because they already knew him from the many letters he had written as a boy.

His "chicken farm" had over 10,000 chickens that laid eggs every day, and these were then sold to the local grocery stores. I could tell you some character building stories about this place and how I shoveled chicken manure (yep, it was really stinky); I shot a "lead mine" at clay pigeons; learned how to speed shift a pickup truck; raised prize winning 4-H Angus steers (which were very tasty); and learned to drive a tractor, rake and bale hay. I was curious about everything.

My father was always trying to help people by creating new jobs in the poverty stricken mountains. During his lifetime, he owned and operated this chicken farm, plus two large coal mines, a dairy farm complete with pasteurizing milk and home milk delivery, and a hog farm. He also raised national "field trial" prize winning bird dogs and fox hounds. None of these were profitable! Medical practice and delivering babies was a full-time job, and there was not enough time to manage a farm and a busy medical practice. But he loved agriculture and nature.

Late in life, he owned a farm which became a wild life habitat for deer, wild turkeys, grouse, quail, ducks, geese, and any other wild animals that happened to pass by. In the last years of their lives, my mother and father would sit in rocking chairs, under a shelter, and watch these wild animals for hours.

I remember talking with him once about how much money he had lost during his lifetime trying to do all these "other" things, and his comment was, "Yep, you are right, I lost a lot of money, but I enjoyed every minute of it." I guess if you look at it that way, it is hard to argue. My mother would disagree with him. But, she was a faithful wife and supported him in whatever he wanted to do.

## Sheriff and Outlaws in the Emergency Room

Growing up as a boy, I remember seeing our sheriff brought into the emergency room of my dad's office. This was the only emergency room we had within 100 miles. This time the sheriff was dead. He had been shot several times in an ambush. He was the first dead man I had seen outside of a funeral home. He was pale gray, blue on the backside, and had blood all over his uniform, with holes and big spots of blood on his chest and abdomen.

He had been ambushed somewhere up in the mountains, and the first place they brought him was "my dad's emergency room." It was the only place we had in the 1950s.

When I was a boy, I remember seeing several law officers who had been shot, (usually over illegal alcohol), terrible car accidents, drownings, shootings, many broken bones sticking out through the skin, heart attacks, and one small boy who had been literally "scalped" when a mule kicked him in the head. I assisted my dad with that one to sew the scalp back on his head. I saw him later and it looked good. You could not even see where he had been scalped. The mule had tried to kick his brains out, but his scalp "hung on."

Sadly, people talk like Family Practice is a lost and dying specialty. But my father could do almost anything. He could set your broken bones, treat your heart attack, trauma, and even deliver your baby. And, he could do it well. When medical malpractice came along, things changed. Nothing got better, it simply drove the cost of medicine through the roof. The lawyers won, and society lost, because today doctors practice "defensive medicine" and order extra expensive tests to avoid lawsuits.

Experience is a great teacher, and few had the experiences he did. All the things you would normally see in a busy emergency department came to this small room in his clinic. It would have made a great medical school! There was lots of pathology!

Our private home was only 20 feet away, and because I was always curious about everything, including medicine, I was in and out of his medical office all the time. Plus my mother would send me to the office to "get your dad for lunch." It seemed he was late more often than he was on time for lunch and supper.

Upstairs in this same "medical office" was the Manchester Maternity Hospital. No… it was not a real hospital as you would think of today, but it was a place where mountain women could come and deliver their babies in safety instead of delivering them at home. It was much safer than home delivery.

I liked being around the medical office. It was interesting as a young boy to see all these things, and my dad was a good teacher. I asked a lot of questions. But I never once got sick or started to pass out when I saw blood.

Only medical people will understand this. As a young boy, I could never figure out what those GYN "speculums" were used for, and my dad would never tell me. It was only in medical school that I learned what pap smears were and how to do pelvic exams. As a child…I was always trying to figure out how they worked! If you are in the medical profession, you are welcome to laugh if you can imagine a little boy playing with one of those speculums, thinking it looked like a duck's bill, and making it go *quack, quack.*

My father was also a Christian. He was not a "believer" when my parents married, and I don't know the exact events that triggered his conversion. But his life was devoted to his family and patients. I have mentioned some of the aspects of his life, because his character deeply affected my own life and character formation.

## Death Was Coming

I had worked for months to build this gas powered model airplane, and today my brother and I were determined to fly it. The paint had finally dried and it was ready.

It was a beauty!

I had painted my model airplane "black" with gold details just like the real Mooney airplane I would own later in life (see photo). The black Mooney paint job was "classy" and I often received nice comments from the control tower when I was landing or taking off. I had named my real Mooney airplane "Amazing Grace -The Wings of Love" and I really enjoyed flying as an instrument rated pilot.

People would often comment about the black color, and say, "You should paint your airplane white because if you have an accident it will be easier to see." My response was, "If I have an accident, I will most likely be dead and it won't matter." But during the summer, I confess it was really hot in that black airplane until you got up to altitude where the temperature dropped.

*My oldest daughter flies with me to Meigs Field in Chicago.*

I hate to fly commercially. Most pilots know what I am talking about. Commercial flying is so boring. Smooth. Seldom a bump, comfortable temperature. You can get up and walk around. They bring you nice cold drinks and a snack. But, in a small plane it is different. It may be boring after you get to altitude and go on auto-pilot, but there are times it can be punctuated with moments of "stark terror," especially in bad weather. I have been there a few times!

So, I started the motor on this small model airplane and gave it to my brother to hold while I ran to pick up the control handle in the center of the circle. In those days we did not have "radio controlled" airplanes, and so, the airplane was controlled with two small steel wires which came out from the wing of the plane and into a red plastic handle which I held in my hand.

The engine was roaring, the wind from the propeller was whipping my brothers t-shirt. I was excited, my heart was already flying. I was nervous but ready to finally fly this airplane. My biggest fear was that he would release it, and I would crash it into the ground and break it into a million pieces! But it felt great to have my fingers wrapped around that control handle, and we were going to "fly" it today or "die trying"!

"Let it go!" I yelled over the roar of the engine. He did, and suddenly the plane was flying! It was great! Round and round and up and down it went. I was so happy.

The airplane was fast and it maneuvered beautifully, I felt like I was "in Heaven"...and little did I know how "real" that possibility was about to become.

Round and round I went, my eyes focused on the plane at the end of the wires. I could see it perfectly, but everything else in the world was a blur as I turned round and round in circles. I flew it up and down, back and forth, but never tried anything too risky.

Then my brother yelled over the engine noise…

"Make it do a loop!"

I hesitated, and then pulled back on the control handle. I remember watching my plane climb, up and up and...

Suddenly...

Nothing…

Inside my head there was an "explosion" of brilliant colors—followed by darkness.

Everything was "gone"…

I only remember the "explosion of colors" then darkness.

I heard "no noise" and felt "no pain."

With great difficulty, I opened my eyes—and discovered that I was paralyzed. I was lying on the ground, unable to breathe, I had no memory of what had happened. I tried to move. I couldn't. Then I realized, *I cannot breathe*, and panic set in.

I heard sounds. But I could barely see through the small slits in my eyes. As though huge lead weights were sitting on top of me, I could not breathe and it felt like I was drowning.

I was terrified!

I wanted to breathe so badly. I tried to "force" myself to take a breath but I couldn't. I knew I "had" to breathe—or die, but I could do nothing but lie there, helpless, waiting to die.

Nothing in my body was moving. My heart pounded like a sledgehammer inside my chest, and I was scared beyond words! I was surrounded, encased, and drowning in a black sea of terror.

This was not a horror movie. It was real. I was *dying*, and there was no way to get up and walk out of this real-life drama.

Then I remember feeling pain....

A *burning* pain…and somehow, I was also on fire!

I could feel my legs burning! And, my arms were burning!

But why? What was going on?

I could not move to get away from the pain or even see why I was burning.

Everything was happening faster than I can write or even than you can read. I was about to die any second, and if something didn't change "*really fast*" I would pass out and be dead in a few more seconds.

With my last bit of consciousness, as my soul slumped toward the unknown depths of death, I prayed…

*Oh God please don't let me die! If you will save me, I will go anywhere you want and do anything you want me to do. Please don't let me die!*

I was begging God for my life!

I know it was a desperate prayer, but I was desperate to live, and it seemed like my only chance. My only hope.

## Several Years Earlier

I was sitting in the back of our small church listening to the preacher say the same things he had said a million times before. God loved us. We were sinners, and Jesus had died for our sins.

It was a Sunday night, and my mother had always made me go to church. I hated it. Even on Sunday nights and Wednesday nights, I had to go. They even forced me to play the piano so people could sing. I wasn't very good, but I got even with them on that one.

When they sang those old "slow" songs, like "Rock of Ages, cleft for me," I would play it at a "fast" tempo and occasionally throw in a few "rock and roll" beats. I remember my uncle who always sang loud and... slow! It was really hard to "speed him up."

Sadly, I must confess to being a very rebellious and stubborn child. Today I am sorry for that and I have apologized to both my parents before they died. I must have made their lives miserable, and I feel so bad about that now. They even sent me off to military school, hoping that would "straighten me out!" But, it didn't work. I came back even more stubborn, rebellious, and aggressive.

*My father and brother with me in uniform at the first military school I attended. The car in the background I totaled when I was driving on a country road with my father.*

*At another military school with me holding my sister's hand.*
*The car in the background I also wrecked as a teenager. Sadly, I*
*was a rebellious boy, which is why I went to military school.*

On Sunday nights, I didn't want to go to church, I wanted to watch the famous *Ed Sullivan Show* on TV and see this new singer called Elvis Presley, or the Beatles, but my mom forced me to go to church even when I didn't want to, which was most of the time.

But on this particular Sunday night, something was different, and the message became real. I understood that even at the age of eleven I **was** a sinner and I **had** done many wrong things. Can you believe that at the age of eleven I was smoking cigarette butts I had stolen from ashtrays? My friends at school were no help, and I was also drinking "moonshine" and riding down the road on the back of a motorcycle with no helmet at 100 mph!

During my teenage years I was shot at with real guns on two different occasions, with sparks flying off the pavement around my feet on one of those occasions. I am ashamed to talk or even think about my early school days now. I was so wrong, and my life was going in the wrong direction.

I was doing a lot of wrong things, even at the age of eleven. I knew it, and that night in the church I understood I was a sinner and would be separated from God forever if I didn't change. When I heard how Christ died for all the wrong things I had done, I began to cry.

When the preacher gave the invitation to come forward and accept Christ, I did. The first step into the aisle was the hardest, but with tears in my eyes I knew I wanted the forgiveness that God was offering, and I didn't care about my friends who were sitting with me. This was between God and me, and I "had" to go forward to the altar.

My mother would tell you she could not believe the change she saw in me the next week. I would agree. I couldn't either! It was not something I had to "force," it just came naturally. Being "born again" is truly a life changing experience. We don't become perfect when we accept Christ as our Savior, but we are changed. We start a new life and begin to do the things that are pleasing to God. Certainly we start a new life, walking, learning, and seeking to be like Christ, and it is never finished until we die.

The following Sunday I was baptized in the river, which ran behind our church and under the new bridge. It was November and quite cold. I don't know how the preacher did it, but he waded out into that cold water, and one after another he baptized three of us. All the way down under the icy water I went, and came up a new person. It felt good. And, no, I never caught a cold or had a sniffle.

When I think back on it, I believe God was "smiling." Because, as I walked out of the water that day, I clearly remember seeing a small crescent of ice at the water's edge. I didn't know it at the time, but God already had plans for me because of "the promise" I would make to Him on this fateful day at the farm.

## My Mother's Prayer and Footsteps

As I lay helpless on the ground in pain, I started to lose consciousness, but I could hear my mother yelling and I felt the ground shaking. It was my mother's footsteps! She was running toward me, as I was dying in this bed of flames....

I could hear her screaming as she ran....

"Jesus, don't take my child!"

"Jesus, don't take my child!"

"Jesus...*please* don't take my child!"

Even today, more than 50 years later, I can still hear my mother's voice crying out to God, and I have difficulty writing those words without tears or being overcome with emotion. I was dying at that very moment.

I have often wondered if it was my prayer and promise that God heard, or the cries of my mother. Maybe both? God loves us more than we can imagine.

My mother had heard what sounded like a loud thunder clap and looked to see what happened. What she saw must have terrified her. Her firstborn son was lying motionless on the ground, in a bed of flames. When she arrived at my paralyzed body, my clothes were on fire and the dry grass all around me was burning.

It didn't matter to her, and in spite of the fire, she did what any good mother would do. She quickly ran into the fire, grabbed my hands and dragged me to a safe place away from the flames and dropped me on the ground. Crying and praying with every step.

When she dropped me on the ground...

...I started to breathe!

I can still recall "gasping" for that first breath of air. It was the violent "gasp" of a drowning person.

But...

*I was going to live!*

I was in pain, my clothes were charred. I smelled like smoke and I was so weak I could not stand or even sit up. But, I was excited to be alive!

I had just flown my model airplane into **30,000 volts of electricity directly over my head.** The electricity "shot" down the metal wires faster than a bullet, passing through my body and into the ground.

The small metal wires melted instantly and rained drops of white hot liquid metal onto the dry grass and set it on fire.

Later, we noticed that the "the electric hit me" while I was taking a step. It entered through the handle in my right hand then exited through my left big toe and right heel. It burned three large holes in my right foot about the size of a quarter, which were later covered with skin grafts and allowed me to walk normally. The red plastic handle in my hand melted, and was deformed from the tetanus grip. I even left perfect fingerprints on the red handle. I had been instantly fried!

Now, each day, when I put on my socks, I see those holes and run my hand over the scars. I thank God for another day and remember the promise I made to Him on that fateful day. I am so thankful for His great mercy to me and for answering my prayer. It is a promise I will never forget, nor fail to keep. God saved my life, and now each new day is a gift that I would never have enjoyed if not for Him.

## The Ambulance Ride to the Emergency Room

The neighbors had already called the local funeral home and ordered a hearse, which is also our local ambulance.

That sounds a bit strange, and maybe a bit humorous, even when I think about it. But no one was laughing that day, and it was "normal" for people who lived in the mountains to use the hearse as our ambulance.

Our ambulance service was the local "undertaker" or funeral director. He was also the coroner for our county. A man who wore several hats quite well.

This accident happened before we had 911, EMTs with emergency services, good ambulances, or even good roads in Eastern Kentucky. This was the 1950s. But our small community had organized an ambulance service, even though there was no government help in those days.

The funeral director had the best equipped vehicle in the county. It had a gurney that could be locked down in the back, plus a siren and flashing emergency lights. No oxygen. No IVs, no defibrillator, but it had "fast drivers" with lots of experience who knew how to drive at high speeds on those "kiss your behind" curvy mountain roads. I never remember any of the funeral home drivers having a wreck. But already, our new 911 ambulance drivers have had several.

My ambulance driver turned out to be a good friend and next door neighbor. He lived only three houses away from me. He was the father of my brother's best friend who later became one of the original founders of Agape Unlimited Inc. and a local pastor. Families and friends are well-known to each other in the remote parts of Appalachia.

Outside of the mountains it is often hard for people to understand the bond that mountain people have. We usually know each other, and it makes us feel like family. It always feels good to see a familiar face. My dad knew everybody, or one of their family members, and they knew him. Always! Sadly, mountain people are also a little "cliquish" to outsiders. But friends, new and old, are always welcome, and the door is never closed.

They loaded me into the hearse, strapped down the gurney, and within seconds we were "flying" around those mountain curves at 90 mph with sirens screaming and emergency lights flashing! It was a dangerous ride to be sure.

In those days, it was common for people to pull over to the side of the road and stop their car out of respect for a funeral procession. I am glad it was not *my* funeral they were being polite for!

I was alive and breathing! Yee Haw…. I was going to live!

## Our Mountain Emergency Room

We arrived at what everyone called the "emergency room" I described earlier. In my small town there was no hospital, and so my dad had equipped one room in his medical office as an emergency room.

After a fast trip into town, we arrived at the emergency room and my dad was waiting for us. He could barely speak he was so emotional. There were no mobile phones in the 1950s for my mother to use, and so the neighbors had called ahead to alert my father and told him that his first-born son had just been electrocuted!

He examined me, and we found the three large charred black places on my feet and red streaks running from my right hand that held the control handle. We could easily follow the red streaks up my right arm and over to the center of my chest, where they forked and went down both my legs. It took more than 10 years for those red streaks to completely disappear!

It looked like at least some of the electric may have followed the path of least resistance, by passing through the sweat on my skin. That may have been one factor that helped save my life and allowed my heart to keep beating, or restart? I also had first- and second-degree burns on my arms and legs from the grass fire.

When the third-degree burns of dead black tissue were removed, we found holes in my right foot that were about one-half inch deep, and each the size of a quarter.

Part of the problem was my "cool dude" attitude. I wore "taps" on the heels of my shoes so that you could hear me coming down the hallway at school a mile away. I was like most teenagers—insecure and wanting to be "noticed."

The electricity exited through each of those three nails. My feet looked and smelled like "burnt BBQ" except with a distinctive "foot" odor that had been added. Later these holes were covered with skin grafts so I could walk normally. But it was *grrreat* to be alive!

Everyone was concerned about the possibility of internal organ damage. But thankfully, nothing ever developed!

I never forgot my promise to God, and the following week, I was in church on crutches. I was "glad" to be there. Both my feet were in bandages and I could barely walk. My muscle strength was still very weak. God had heard my prayer and allowed me to live.

Each time I put on my socks my hands rub across those holes, and I thank God for another day. We should never take any day God gives us for granted! It is so precious and is filled with opportunities to share His Love with others.

Psalm 139:16 says, "God has planned all the days of our life from before we were formed in our mother's womb…" But at the time, I was too young to know that.

Still, every day when I unwrapped those bandages to soak my feet in the warm soapy water, I could smile. I was thankful to be alive and breathing.

CHAPTER TWO

# promises...promises... promises

## Yes, I Remember the Promise

many years later during the last year of my surgical residency, I was sitting in church on a Sunday night, listening to a missionary from Africa. He was showing us slides of the hungry, naked, starving children, when suddenly the Holy Spirit grabbed my heart by surprise. God was reminding me of the promise I had made many years ago, and asking, "Are you going to keep your promise to me...or not?"

As the tears welled up in my eyes and flowed down my cheeks, His hand was squeezing my heart to respond to the invitation that was being given by the missionary to "go." I was in His grip like grapes in a winepress, and I was remembering "the promise" I had made many years before.

Would I keep my promise and "GO"…

Or not?

Respond? Now? Did God seriously want me to give up my surgical career? I would be finished in a couple of months. If I quit now, I would lose everything I had worked and studied for. But God continued to squeeze my heart. He wanted to know "if" I would "GO" on the mission field, **today,** not tomorrow, but **NOW!**

The urgency of God. Sometimes, it is so hard to understand. Abraham took Isaac and left the next morning. Not much time to think about that… Just obey and saddle the donkey.

But, I knew…that if I said "NOT NOW"…God would go away and leave me alone, and He would not trouble me with this again. I also knew that if that happened, I would lose my nearness and my intimacy with Him. (If you are not a believer, you probably cannot understand that statement. I am sorry.) I didn't want that, because life for me without "oneness" with God would be meaningless and useless, and nothing would be worth that price.

I could not sit still. I had to decide. Would I give up everything I had worked and studied for "right now" to become "entirely His" so that He could use me in His service?

It was "now or never." But… Lord, I had invested so many, many long years of sleepless nights, study, and hard work to get to this point. And now, you are asking me to "throw it all away." This "doesn't make any sense." "Why would you ask me to do this *now*?"

I only had a few more seconds before the invitation would be finished….

But, I wanted that nearness with God more than anything in the world. So, I choose to go forward and confirm that "**I would keep**

**my promise"** and **"go" anywhere He wanted**. I was HIS, and He could use me any way He wanted! Anytime He wanted.

It was a hard decision, and my eyes were filled with tears. It was different this time. I was **not** dying, it was not the desperate prayer of a dying teenager struggling for breath, but a voluntary "decision" of my own free will that I was making to God. I didn't have to make it, but I *chose* to do it.

"You shall be careful to do what has passed your lips, for you have **voluntarily** vowed to the LORD your God what you have promised with your mouth" (Deut. 23:23, ESV).

I understood God had called me to be "His." But... Where? At that moment, I thought it would be Africa. There was no hint of "anything" related to Russia. **But I always understood that my call was to "God" Himself, and not a place!** God would always be with me no matter where I went, and my part was to simply trust and obey Him.

I went forward at the invitation, and afterward talked with the missionary. He advised me to finish my surgical residency, and then go into missions. It was a huge emotional relief to hear that, but I was willing to leave that night if necessary. Later when I finished my surgical residency, I probably "deceived" myself by deciding that God wanted me to be a missionary in Appalachia. I justified the decision by saying that I already spoke the "mountain" language, understood the culture, and the people who lived there were poor and needed help.

There were a lot of factors involved in that decision, one of which was that I had married a Christian lady in the last month of my surgical residency, and I was anxious to be a good husband and provide for my new family.

I moved to Appalachia and started working night and day to provide for my family and serve God. But within a few years, deep emotional problems unknown to me were taking place in the marriage.

## Promises... Promises... Promises

We all make them!

Husband and wife make them before God and witnesses. Business partners make them when they sign contracts. Governments make them when they sign treaties. We make promises to our children. Our teachers, our friends, our families, etc. Our life is filled with promises.

The consequences of broken promises are easily seen in our lives, and the lives of others. Divorce, drug addiction, adultery, lust, greed, lying, stealing, bitterness, hate, etc. are all the result of a broken promise somewhere along the way.

Statistics show that about 50% of us have broken our vows to our spouse as evidenced by marriage unfaithfulness and the divorce rate.

It hurts to stay in a marriage when things are not going right.

But according to Jesus, "…He who created them from the beginning made them male and female, and said, 'Therefore a man shall leave his father and his mother and hold fast to his wife, and the two shall become one flesh.' So they are no longer two but one flesh. What therefore God has joined together, let not man separate" (Matt 19:4-6, ESV).

Divorce is a disaster for everyone involved.

If you are thinking about divorce, I encourage you to seek Godly counseling. Usually divorce will cause a lot of pain and suffering to everyone involved, especially the children, and statistics show that both sides are usually worse off five years after the divorce. Many times if you will be patient, and seek help, it gets better. Life is constantly changing, and sometimes a little time is needed to solve the problem.

So, "why" do we break our promises?

The answer is simple: "We are selfish."

We would rather satisfy our passions and desire for personal pleasure than to keep our promises to God and others. "Me first, everybody else last."

Most of us will break a significant vow or promise during our lifetime, and sadly, the people who love us most will suffer.

But, the good news is that God **always** keeps His promises. He never fails!

"Not one word of all the good promises that the LORD had made to the house of Israel had failed; all came to pass" (Joshua 21:45, ESV).

Feelings come and go. And it is important to remember that *true love* is not just a feeling but action, such as when Jesus walked up Calvary! That is "true love"!

Have you ever sacrificed like that for someone you loved (even though they didn't love you in return)? If so, you understand more about love than most people on this planet.

Looking back at the electrical accident and the promise I made, I can see God's hand weaving the circumstances of my life together to give me a choice, whether I would keep my promise and obey Him or not.

We tend to think that doing it God's way will result in disaster. But God is still running the Universe, and He has not made any mistakes that I am aware of. If you feel He has made a mistake, I encourage you to discuss it with Him.

You do **not** have faith, as long as you are standing firmly on the ground of common sense. You must step off into the "abyss of the unknown." If there is no "action" and no jump…there is no faith (James 2: 14-18).

But, would I "really" keep my promise to God?

Would I "really" leave everything and "GO" to Russia?

At this point in my life, only God knew…

But there was still one "*HUGE*" question to be answered…

**Would God keep His promise to me?**

I believed He would… but, the only way to know for sure was "to jump."

Would He catch me, or would I crash and burn?

# CHAPTER THREE

# character formation in the appalachian soul

*Me (L), my father (C), and my younger brother riding horses in Appalachia.*

## My Father's Life Was a Huge Influence in Shaping Mine

We do not choose our parents, or where we want to be born. God does that. I think He did a good job, because I was blessed to have good parents who loved me, helped me throughout my life, and most importantly, they taught me about God.

Nevertheless, the culture instilled in me a proud mountain heritage and a strong family bond. Some would say I have a stubborn "hillbilly" attitude, and it would be hard for me to say they are wrong.

Mountain people are generally very strong, family oriented people, but… stubborn. I hope I have not offended family or friends with that statement, but I think it is "generally" true.

Therefore, we had many feuds in Eastern Kentucky because of family loyalties. The History Channel once did a documentary about the biggest feud in the USA. It was in my county, and it was much larger and more deadly than the famous Hatfield and McCoy's feud in West Virginia.

People often think mountain people are stupid and ignorant, and some are, but many have a "common sense" and practical approach to things that the rest of the world could learn from.

God does not make mistakes. We are what we are by the love and mercy of God, and He has a plan for each of our lives even before we are born (Psalm 139:16).

Even if you were born in a "yurt" in Siberia or in a teepee on the frozen Russian Tundra, God has a purpose and plan for your life. He doesn't make mistakes in running the Universe. But, sometimes I have to admit, His ways are really hard to understand. I guess that is where faith comes in and logic leaves.

Since we do not choose our parents or where we are born… complaining doesn't help. My best advice is that if you are in a place

*Riding horses again, but this time in Siberia.*

you don't like, remember the beautiful lily, and bloom wherever God plants you. If you do, people will notice and wonder, "How do you do it?"

I was blessed because God gave me two Godly parents. If you were shot or injured, as many were, my father was usually the first doctor to see you. During his lifetime, he delivered more than 10,000 babies, three generations of children, before he died at the age of 96.

He was a patriarch in our community, and because he was my father, his life impacted me—deeply.

Eastern Kentucky is a poor part of America, and so many of my childhood school friends had no indoor bathrooms. Their houses were often heated with "pot belly" or "warm morning" coal stoves, and the kitchen stoves burned wood for cooking. But those mountain women could make some of the best mouth-watering biscuits and gravy or cornbread you ever ate on those wooden stoves. I guess it is no surprise that the country cooking at Cracker Barrel restaurants has become a huge success, even though they don't use wood burning stoves.

It was amazing how often I heard my father giving "spiritual advice" to unmarried teenage girls, "moonshiners," and outlaws. Yep, real outlaws, who would kill you just because you came from the wrong family. My father knew many outlaws, because he went to school with some of them and was raised in a very tough area. I remember he would often express his concern to my mom that "those little 13 year old girls are too young to know how to be mothers."

## Guns, Mountain Culture and the Value of Life

Guns were always a huge part of my childhood. Today, you often read in the news about children going to school and shooting other children. I, and nearly all my classmates, were raised around guns. We knew how to use them, where they were located in the house, how to load, unload, and shoot them. No one "ever" thought about going to school and using them to kill people. I am convinced the problem with guns is more social than anything. Our country has changed dramatically in culture and morals over the past 50 years, and to a degree these moral and cultural changes are reflected by our changing society.

It seems that the "value of human life" is less today than it was in my childhood. In those days, it was rare to hear of a girl having an abortion in our community. I don't remember ever hearing of anyone in our community getting an abortion. There probably were, but I never heard about it. Everyone knew that a pregnancy was an unborn child…. And so, you got married and worked it out.

No, those marriages didn't automatically fail. I know several couples who have been married for many years and without a divorce. They seem to be as happy as any other married couple after they worked through the shame and deep emotions that come with an unwanted pregnancy. It's funny how a newborn baby can change hearts when people hold it in their arms.

It is interesting to note that marriages have been "arranged" for centuries in Eastern countries, and their divorce rates are often less than in the West. Life was precious to most women who lived in the mountains. Even if that life started as an "accident."

My father believed life was sacred. I remember meeting a man who told me how my father saved his life. He came to our small hospital ER and died. My father "**never** gave up" on human life, or trying to save it. He defibrillated this man's heart nearly 20 times. As a doctor it was his responsibility to do everything possible to save a life. Today, in our post modern world, that moral conviction is hard to find.

Anyway, this man told me that he was glad my father "shocked" him **18 times** to bring him back to life. The hospital staff wanted to quit and give up several times. They kept telling my dad it was hopeless to continue. Pull the plug, stop the CPR, but my father would not. The man lived many years after that with no evidence of any brain injury. The motto "never give up" also applies to human life.

## Family Security: There Was Always a Gun Next to Our Door

As young children growing up, we all developed a strong sense of family loyalty. If you tried to physically harm my father's family, he would not think twice about shooting you! In fact, he probably would not even think about it at all!

He kept a loaded gun by the door, "just in case," so that when he answered the door at 2 a.m. it would be there, if it was needed, and sometimes it was.

He always used a gun as an "equalizer," never to be an aggressor. I remember one summer night hearing a "drug addict" arguing with my father through my open upstairs window. He was insisting that my father give him "medicines" (drugs). The more he talked, the more aggressive he became, because my father would not give him the drugs. During the arguing, my father showed him the pistol and said, "Now go away, I don't want any trouble with you." After that, the man left and I heard my father call the local sheriff. In a few minutes they arrested

*"Me" pretending to be a cowboy.*

him not far from our house. (I could see red and blue lights flashing through my bedroom windows.)

In all his 96 years, my father never shot anyone, and maybe he was more "bluff" than anything, but it would not have been a good idea to test him. He always said that he didn't want to shoot anyone, "Because…then I would have to stop and "fix 'em." But, make no mistake about it, if you threatened him or his family, he would shoot you…with a .44 magnum! And… You don't usually get up after that.

The news only tells stories about how guns kill people. But guns can also save lives when a young mother is protecting her children, or an elderly lady is being assaulted and robbed or, in one case, my elderly father.

As I said before, he always kept a loaded .44 magnum pistol in his home, usually under the TV set, next to the door. All the children knew where it was. We knew it was loaded, even the grandchildren knew, and no one ever bothered it. When young children came to visit, he would always put it away and out of reach. All of our family knew how to use a gun, even my mother.

When my father was about 90 years old, he once needed his gun to even the odds against some young hoodlums. He owned a 385 acre farm that was remotely located high up in the mountains, and at the head of a holler. After you leave the asphalt of a backcountry road, you travel along a dirt road that clings to the side of a mountain, slowly curving around the hills and inching upward for about 3 miles. It is a one-lane road. You don't drive fast because you can't. And, if you go over the edge, it is a long way to the bottom of the mountain.

He went to this farm nearly every afternoon after he finished work at the medical office. He often went alone. It was his way to relax and watch the deer, turkey, birds, and wildlife. He loved to be outdoors, and some of the fondest memories I have of my father is when we went "fox hunting" on Friday night at this farm, or another placed called "Sacker." It was almost a religious event for him on Friday after work, and I have some wonderful memories of our times together.

This is the story my father told us after he came home one day from the farm.

On this particular afternoon when he arrived at the farm, he noticed three strange men walking around near the barn. There was no one else there but him and these three strangers. This is a one lane road, and he couldn't turn around. He drove his truck up near where they were standing and started talking to them. They started to laugh and make fun of this "old man" and began walking toward him in a threatening way, talking about what they were going to do to him.

My father reached over and picked up his .44 magnum pistol that was next to him in the pickup, raised it up high enough for them to see, and set it on the truck's dashboard. Then he said, "Boys, I don't want no trouble, so don't start any. You don't belong up here, this is private property, so start walking down this road and get off this farm. Don't be foolish and make me have to shoot you." At that point, they started walking down the road, where they were met by the sheriff about 20 minutes later who was coming up the road. My father had already called the sheriff on his shortwave radio.

The pistol certainly saved my dad from getting beat up, injured, or possibly killed. On this particular day it was an "equalizer" between a frail elderly man and three young criminals who were planning to hurt him.

## Fox Hunting: Time for Bonding and Fun

On Friday afternoons after office hours, we would get into our separate 4x4 trucks, load about 20 fox hounds into the back of his pickup, and off we went up the side of a mountain, slipping and sliding in four-wheel drive, and occasionally getting stuck in the mud. Then we would hook a chain to the other truck and pull each other back onto solid ground; fun, but muddy and dirty.

Once we reached the top of the hill, we would build a fire, even if it was raining. About the edge of dark we "let the dogs out"!

When you opened the tailgate on the truck…it was "Katie…bar the door!" The dogs would be jumping everywhere. All over each other, and you, trying to get out of the truck. They knew the "fun" was about to start!

Then we would cook supper, talk and laugh with other fox hunters who joined us. These men would sit there and listen all night to the dogs barking as they traveled up and down the mountains and across the valleys. You could hear the dogs bark for miles in the stillness of the cool mountain air.

Each person around the fire would then try to convince the others that his dog was leading the chase. And, yes, each person knew the sound of their dog's bark, just like a mother would recognize her baby's cry in the nursery!

"Listen…that's ole Goosejaw out in front…." one would say.

"Nope, that's Maggie Brown…" another would say.

Then if the others didn't agree, they would argue about it. The laughing and arguing was all part of the fun.

Not all the dogs barked at once, only the lead dog would bark when on a hot trail and the others would then join in behind it.

I don't know where they came up with the names for their dogs. Some of the names were comical or funny, and I don't think there was any logic to it. My father once had a national field trial champion that was named "Hey You." Good name...I never forgot it! And I suppose if you were in the field and couldn't remember your dog's name then .... "Hey You" would be a good choice.

These were good memories. We never killed a single fox! You were not supposed to. The plan was to get to the top of the mountain, build a fire, cook supper, and join the fellowship with other fox hunters around the fire. After supper we would sit back, relax, whittle on a stick, spit (many fox hunters chew tobacco), and listen to the dogs bark.

I seldom stayed the full night, but my father would usually find a bed or sleep in the front seat of his truck. But I usually came off the hill and went home about midnight.

Since we were both doctors and worked at the local hospital, we had shortwave radios in our trucks (nice). The hospital would call us for instructions about patients we had in the hospital. If there was a shooting or an emergency, then I had to come off the mountain and go back to the ER, usually a 20-30 minute drive if I didn't get stuck.

## Dead Sheriffs, Moonshine, and Mountain Feuds

This was the culture I was raised in. Mountain people are hardworking and don't like to be made fun of. Their word was their bond and business was often concluded on a handshake. Many books and stories have been written about the feuds in West Virginia, Kentucky, North Carolina and Tennessee. As I mentioned previously, the most well-known is probably the "Hatfield and McCoy" feud in West Virginia. But by far one of the bloodiest feuds in the USA took place in my home county in Eastern KY.

The feud was between the "Whites and the Bakers." It was so bad that the "militia" from the state capital was sent to keep order so the court could try the case without anyone being killed. It didn't help much since the main character in the feud, who was on trial, was shot and killed coming out of the courthouse...while the army was camped on the courthouse lawn! They found the rifle but never found or caught the killer. Mountain men are usually good shots. I was too, as most of us were.

Sadly, the Eastern seaboard press loved our mountain feuds, and often exaggerated them to make a good story. This is one reason why, even today, many people from the mountains do not like the news media.

You can find more information in many books, and on the web about this feud. It was sad. So many sons on both sides were lost because of "hate." For more information, simply search the web for the Baker and White feud in Kentucky.

The shootings in our area were usually about "bootlegging," moonshine, money or family quarrels. You see, I lived in what we call a "dry county." No alcoholic beverages could be bought or sold "legally," so bootleggers made huge profits from the sale of illegal alcohol. If the sheriff started to cause problems, they usually killed him or he would decide to take a bribe and leave them alone.

These outlaws had no guilt about killing people. They would often wait in the mountains to ambush the sheriff's car as it drove by. They were hard core, unemotional, downright "mean" men. I used the term "mean" because I can't think of a better term. They were a sad disgrace to our part of the world, but nevertheless a constant part of it.

### Screaming Women…All Night Long!

My father was an excellent family doctor and delivered three generations of children. Most of them were born in a special part of the upstairs medical office that he called "The Manchester Maternity Hospital." As I said before, it was not a hospital as you think of one today. It was simply a place where mountain women could come and stay to have their babies safely.

As a child I had no idea what "the delivery room" was, and for sure, I had no idea what they were "delivering" in there, or what went on. It was a strange and mysterious place for a young boy.

I only remember it as my dad's "maternity hospital" and, as a child, I had no idea what the word "maternity" meant. Sadly, this place was only a few feet from our front door. My brother and I would often play in the front yard under a huge maple tree, which was about 20 feet away from the "delivery room." Summer was the worst time, because we could hear women screaming while we played in the yard…and then a baby would cry. We were too young to understand it.

This was in the days before "epidurals" and my brother and I never really understood what all the screaming was about until we were much older. It was "normal" for us as children to hear women screaming, day or night, and continue to play as if nothing was happening. Heck, they could have been killing people in there and we would never have known it.

In the summertime, it was always hot and humid and my bedroom was on the second floor on the opposite end of the house from the office. During those hot days, the windows were always open, and we had a window fan that ran all season. There were NO air conditioners in those days! Isn't that amazing?!

It was hard to sleep during those awful hot humid nights, and we soon got used to a familiar pattern. We would hear the screen door downstairs "slam," the *slap, slap, slap* of our dad's house shoes on the sidewalk, the screen door to the office would "slam," a woman would be screaming and screaming and screaming, and then not too long after he went inside, we would hear a baby cry. It was hard to sleep during those nights! Poor neighbors!

I remember when we installed a new window air conditioner. It was so great! We closed the windows, and after that we couldn't hear the screaming so much. Having babies must be a painful experience!

You have to remember this was 50 years ago, before modern day anesthesia, and childbirth *was* a painful experience. It for sure made me appreciate what my mother went through to give birth to me and my brother and sister!

## I Hated Breaking Green Beans! (and still do!)

Every summer my mother forced (yes, it was forced slavery!) her children to sit under a large shade tree in our front yard and break up bushels and bushels and bushels, and what seemed like truckloads of green beans from the garden to put in the freezers. This was food for the women who came to the "Maternity Hospital" to have their babies! (I forgot to mention the bushels and bushels and bushels of fresh corn on the cob she also put in the freezer.)

The hospital had several rooms for the mothers before and after delivery, plus a labor and delivery room. Since it was upstairs over my father's medical office and 20 feet from our door, it was handy for delivering babies and seeing patients without the need to drive to a hospital far away. Very convenient, but impossible today!

Can you imagine, every summer my mother would fill three large chest freezers full of green beans, corn, and garden vegetables. Later she would cook the food in our small kitchen to feed the women who came to the "maternity hospital" to have their babies. Believe me, it was better tasting and better quality food than you can get in any hospital today! But, the government would never allow good home-cooked meals in a hospital today. Everyone talked about how good the food was, and no one ever got sick, only fatter.

Today, I still hate breaking green beans. During those hot summers, with no air conditioning, the smallest of breezes was so refreshing. After we finished "stringing and breaking" the beans, my mom would need to "blanche" the beans and corn for the freezer. All the burners on our electric stove were on high, so during the summer our house was "hotter than h---" if I can use that expression. Sorry, I can't think of a better way to describe it.

Because the house was so hot, I couldn't wait to get outside. I can still hear my mother's voice yelling behind me as I ran outside to play... "Don't slam the screen door!" I think all mothers in those days had special training to say that, because I heard the same from women who were not my mother. Can you believe there was a time when people didn't have TV or air conditioning? Yes, we had lots of flies too. The good news is that my family had indoor bathrooms while many of my school friends did not.

Because our home was near the medical office, people came to our house day and night, 24/7/365 to ask for help. Knocking on the door at 2 and 3 a.m. was no surprise. It happened often and was part of our normal life. In summer, through our open windows, my brother and I could hear our father talking to a patient in the wee hours of the morning. We would wake up, roll over and go back to sleep. We were never afraid of drunks, terrorists, or drug addicts. As I said before, my dad always had a loaded gun near the door, and I "NEVER" saw or heard him refuse help to anyone, even at 2 a.m., whether they had paid their medical bills or not. We knew this, because often the conversation started with, "Doc, I am sorry I haven't paid my bill, but…"

"Medicine" was his "calling" instead of a business as it is now. Today, most of the compassionate physicians are gone, and sadly, medicine is about money. People call this progress.

I remember hearing people say, "If you think the government will take care of you, look what they did for the American Indian." It seems to still be true today, in all countries, and with all governments. Governments are run by people. Some are kind and compassionate, others are not. Our world has not changed much over the centuries.

## The Golden Age of Medicine

My father practiced medicine in what I call the "golden age" of medicine, because medical care was between a compassionate doctor and his patient. Sometimes patients paid their bills, many times they did not, but our family never starved, and we were blessed with everything we needed and more.

As you can imagine, sometimes we were paid in farm products. It was especially nice if we received a "country ham," which is still one of my favorite foods: Biscuits, country ham and eggs with "red eye" gravy. This is so good, "Your tongue will slap your brains out wanting more," as Jeff Foxworthy would say.

The "golden age" of medicine was a time when doctors and patients had a close relationship with each other.

When the knock on the door would wake me up, I could hear people say things like... "Doc, our little baby has been sick for a week, can you take a look at her? She is really sick with a high temperature and we couldn't get here any sooner...."

Many times they had traveled out of a holler deep in the mountains, sometimes crossing rivers, riding mules, wagons, and jeeps to get here. Most did not have a car and depended upon their neighbors to bring them to the doctor. So, it was often impossible for them to get a ride into town, except late in the evening after their neighbors or friends had finished working and had eaten supper.

He cared about his patients, and he "knew" his patients. All of them! He would say, "Now…whose girl (boy) are you?" Meaning, who are your parents? Again, I never remember him refusing to treat a patient if they did not have money.

Because he knew his patients, sometimes he did talk pretty "rough" (straight) to them…. And I remember our family was often embarrassed to hear him do that. Usually it was more "chastisement" for not coming sooner, instead of coming in the middle of the night.

He was a very unusual person, in that he "loved" the practice of medicine and enjoyed helping people more than anyone I ever met. We sometimes thought he loved medicine more than his family. But, he was blessed to have my mother who always supported him even in some of the "crazy" ideas he often had. I would say, she "spoiled" him.

He was loved and respected by the people in Southeastern Kentucky. Our regional health department is named in his honor. He was past president of the Kentucky Chapter of the Academy of Family Physicians; he was chief of medicine and chief of staff at our local hospital. He was given the "Senior Star Award" from Center on Aging by Senator Bob Dole and was awarded the "Physician Community Service Award" from the Kentucky Medical Association. He loved medicine, and everyone who met him knew it.

He was always learning new things by keeping up with his CME (continuing medical education), even during the last years of his life. Before he died at the age of 96, he could tell you the latest medicines and treatments for cardiac disease, hypertension, and other common diseases. Not only did he know them, but he practiced them. Maybe this is one reason why he lived to be 96? He took his medicines every day!

## What Is It?

I remember once when there were two of us younger doctors gathered around a sick child with a rash. We had no idea what the problem was. Yes, it's true doctors don't know everything! The child had a high temperature and was seriously sick. We invited my father to examine the child and get his opinion. He walked into the room, took out his stethoscope, listened to the chest, looked at the child's rash and said, "Open your mouth," and laughed! "This child has measles!" he said and left. None of us had ever seen a case of measles before, because today we vaccinate against it! There is no substitute for experience!

Everywhere he went, whether it was to a local restaurant, "fox hound show," or cross country wagon ride, he was well-known and respected by the people in his community.

## Home Calls: Mules, Wagons, Jeeps, Rivers, Boats and...Mud!

In the afternoons during my childhood my father always made "home calls." I hated them! He serviced three large mountain counties with his medical practice, and always carried his "little black bag" everywhere he went.

One of those counties was the poorest in the state of Kentucky and fourth poorest in the United States at the time. It is hard to imagine poverty being worse than some of the places we went on "home calls." Many places did not have electric lights and none of them had running water or indoor bathrooms.

I remember on many occasions my dad sitting on the bed of a sick person with a "coal oil" lamp (kerosene) nearby on the table while he examined the patient.

He once told us stories about how he and my mother delivered babies by "coal oil" lamp while the chickens were roosting in the rafters overhead. My mother would hold the flashlight for the delivery. I don't know how they did it. Whenever I delivered babies or did C-Sections, it seems like I **never** had enough "light." I guess we should "not" call those the "good ole days," and be thankful that our "new days" are a lot better!

## One "Home Call" to a Family in the Mountains

As a child, I remember one home call in particular where we drove to the county line, which was about an hour from our house. We were to meet some people who would take us across the river and up to their house on a nearby mountain farm. After we parked the car, my father blew the car horn. The county line was the river. We waited. It was now dark.

After about 15 minutes I saw some lights across the river, and two men got into a very small boat and paddled across the river to where we were parked. We got out of the car and walked down the riverbank. It was my job to carry his "little black bag." (It didn't feel so little at the time!)

The men wanted to be helpful and carry his medical bag, to which I had no objection and was grateful. To a small boy that "little black bag" seemed to weigh a ton.

Our riverbanks were always slick, and it was very easy to fall and slide down the bank and into the water. Been there, done that! My mother didn't like it either. The riverbanks in our part of the world were muddy and not "sandy" like a beach. It was always a mess, and the mud was like glue or cement that always stuck to your shoes. After two steps you were walking on the mud that stuck to your shoes, and it would feel like you had a hard rock in the center of your foot. You could easily feel the difference. It was hard to keep your balance and not fall down.

After we stepped into this undersized boat and sat down, the men paddled to the opposite side. I wasn't sure the little boat would make it. It was what we call a "Jon" boat. The bottom is flat, and so it only needs

*Our Medical Team crossing a river in*
*Northern Russia. Notice the shallow boat.*

a few inches of water to float. It literally feels like you are sitting on top of the water, because you are.

Many years later, I saw this same principle used in boats on Siberian Rivers. Water was just inches away, so I sat very "still" to keep from rocking the boat. There was already too much water in the boat and it quickly covered the soles of my shoes and made my socks wet. We didn't need any more water in the boat.

The men had brought kerosene lanterns and flashlights to show the path on this moonless night. There were no streetlights or electricity to help us see. But the part that bothered me the most was all the water "inside" the boat! I thought we were going to sink before we got to the other side! While one man paddled, the other would "bail" water with an old, rusty Maxwell House coffee can and, of course, we didn't sink. They used these boats nearly every day to fish with what we call "trot lines." These are long fishing lines with many hooks and bait on them that stretched across the river.

It was past dark when we got out of the boat, climbed up the other bank, slipping and sliding in the mud. My dad and these men seemed like professionals to me. I was slipping and sliding, and almost fell down, when suddenly one of the men reached out, grabbed my hand and pulled me up onto solid ground.

We climbed up into an old wooden farm wagon pulled by a team of mules. There was no ladder, so you stepped onto the hub of the wagon wheel, then the rim, and finally into the wagon. I did that part okay. Have you ever harnessed a mule or horse to a wagon? If so, you know it is a huge job!

In Eastern KY, most people did not use horses for farm work because everyone said that a mule was stronger and would work longer than a horse. But, as everyone knows, it is a lot more stubborn.

If you are an evolutionist, it will help you to understand that "evolution" doesn't work, at least on a farm. All farm boys know that a mule is a cross between a "jack" (donkey) and a horse, and that the offspring (a mule) is sterile and doesn't reproduce. So much for the theory of evolution. The species line appears to be very strong, and so cats and dogs, etc. can't crossbreed.

I sat in the back of the wagon, and now it was dark. I felt every bump and rock in the road because as I remember this wagon did not have any springs. If it did, they didn't work. Many years later I found out that riding in a Russian jeep is much the same as riding in a wooden farm wagon. There was no moon. No streetlights. No city lights, and barely enough light to see the trail. It was "dark."

It was autumn, and my nose felt cold and wet. The men talked with my dad about farming, cows, horses, fox hunting, etc. while the mules slowly pulled us toward the farmhouse. I forgot to mention that in the mountains we also like mules because they remind us of our relatives, who are also really stubborn.

## Grandma Is Dying

About thirty minutes after we crossed the river and drove up the holler, we arrived at the house. There was no electricity, only the warm yellow glow of the kerosene lamps. Several of the "kinfolk" had already gathered at the old farmhouse, because everyone knew that grandma was dying. There were old and young people, as well as babies, because family ties run deep and strong in the mountains of Appalachia. Families are the one thing everyone had, no matter how rich or poor you were. We all had a family. We were proud of some of our family members, but others…well, we didn't mention them much.

To me, it seemed like a 'big" house, but in those days it was not uncommon for women to have eight to ten children and some children would usually die during infancy. So, you needed a big house to raise a large family to work a mountain farm. Most of the family was here tonight.

The house was old, but practical, and of course it was not "nice" by today's standards. It had no central heat or air conditioning, but it had those typical tall farmhouse windows, squeaky unpainted floorboards, and coal burning stoves and fireplaces.

The room where grandmother was lying in bed had a fireplace that provided both heat and light for the dimly lit room. I am sure this old grandmother was happy to be at home with all her children and grandchildren gathered around her. She was dying and everyone knew it, and she did too.

She had a high fever, and the family was doing all the "usual" things you would see in a movie. They had washcloths folded across her forehead, and they would wipe her face with cool wet towels from a washbasin nearby. She was moaning with every breath.

The room had a distinct recognizable odor. It was Vicks VapoRub. For some reason it seems like all our old folks in this part of the country always rubbed this stuff on their chest when they were sick. It was very common. I have no idea whether it helped or not…but you could always smell the Vicks before you entered the room. My grandmother's house also smelled this way.

There was a "coal" fire burning in the fireplace, and you could smell the sulfur long before arriving at the house. People almost never used wood for heating their homes. We lived in a coal mining community and coal was readily available and cheaper than wood. Coal also burns hotter and longer than wood, but it does give off a strong characteristic sulfur smell.

The problem with a coal fire is removing the "clinkers." Clinkers are the fused "rock ash" that is left when coal finishes burning. People often throw this on a dirt path to keep it from being so muddy. But, the sharp edges of the rock ash can cut your shoes to shreds if you are not careful.

When I entered the room, I instantly felt the warmth of the fireplace on my face. It felt good after riding in the cold damp air. I looked around for a place to set "the little black bag." But, before I could set it down, my father had already taken it from my hand.

I watched and listened with curiosity as he talked to the lady. He spoke in low, unhurried tones to ask questions about how long she had been sick. Did she have a cough, had they seen any blood, when did she get sick, etc.?

As I looked around at the others in the room, all eyes were on "the doctor" and what he was doing and saying. Mothers would leave the room when their children became "fussy," and so the only sound in the dimly lit room was the crackling of the fire and my father's voice. He was the "center of attention," and everyone was interested to know what was going to happen. It was a real life drama.

The soft glow of the kerosene lamps made it hard to see, but my father took her blood pressure, listened to her chest with a stethoscope, and "thumped" on her chest as all the old physicians often did, and then announced to everyone that she had pneumonia and he was going to give her a "shot" of penicillin. He never gave "injections"... only "shots."

## Penicillin, the Miracle Drug

Can you imagine what it feels like to give the first injection of a new miracle drug called penicillin? My father remembers. Penicillin has saved millions of lives and is still widely used today in many parts of the world.

My father told me the story of a small girl who was dying of Rheumatic Fever in a small mission hospital in our county. He had learned about this new "miracle drug" at a medical conference he had recently attended. So, he called the only medical University we had in our state and "begged" them for Penicillin for this child. They agreed, and he immediately got in his car and drove eight hours to get the medicine and bring it back. He returned home the same day and gave it to her that night.

In those days, travel was a real adventure, and people were often involved in car accidents. The roads were a lot different than the interstate system today. There were many "head-on" collisions from coming around a mountain curve. He traveled about 200 miles each way over muddy mountain roads out of the hollers of Eastern Kentucky, and finally up to the University located in the "big city." There was no FedEx or UPS in those days. The medicine, he said, saved the life of this small child.

He went on to tell me that penicillin was so "precious," it was recrystallized from the urine and used again. Can you believe that? Doctors would collect the urine, "recrystallize" the penicillin and re-inject it! When he told me this, I didn't believe him until I looked it up! As it turns out this was a common practice when penicillin was rare and in short supply, and there are many medical journal references to support this practice.[2]

His "little black medical bag" always seemed to contain everything a doctor could possibly need. It had syringes, needles, scalpels, hemostats, suture material, antibiotics, nitroglycerine, aspirin, and medicines of all colors, shapes and sizes. No wonder it was so heavy! I was carrying around a doctor's office! It seemed so heavy, I would have sworn there was an x-ray machine in there!

The bag always seemed lighter on the way back, not because he used a lot of medicines and supplies but because I was young and tired, and he would often carry it part of the way back to the car. Later, after we returned to the office, he would give the bag to his nurses and they would re-stock the bag with medicines and supplies.

I hated "home calls" when I was a boy. It kept me from playing with my friends, and doing the things "I" wanted to do. Sadly, I never realized

2    Fraser I. Penicillin: *Early Trials in War Casualties*. Br Med J (Clin Res Ed). 1984;289:1723–1725

at the time how valuable and precious those memories would become. But they left a deep impression on me about what it means to be a compassionate and caring doctor. Those memories were instrumental in shaping the person I became later in life.

I can still remember seeing my dad draw up that white penicillin into a glass syringe in the yellow glow of those kerosene lamps. I don't know how he did it...I could barely see, it was so dark. He never needed glasses except for reading, and even in his old age could spot a deer or wild animal quicker than most people.

I don't know "how much" penicillin he gave this sick woman, but as a child it seemed to me like "an awful lot." At least, I wouldn't want that much penicillin injected in me! I don't think I could walk! Not only that, but I was shocked to see him give her, not one, but two shots, one in each butt (hip).

Sitting on the edge of the bed, he announced to the family that she should be better in a "couple of days" and if not, they should come and get him again.

Finally, he closed up his little black bag, handed it to me, and we started home. Now, it was really dark, and crossing the river was not as easy as before, but thankfully, I never "slipped" and fell into the water, and our trip home was peaceful and quiet. It was late and I was also tired.

When we arrived home, my mother said, "Don't forget to wipe your muddy feet..." But, they were *always* muddy...or smelling bad! She didn't need to look!

Today, I have fond memories of making those "home calls" up the mountain hollers with my father, and I am ashamed of my stubborn and disrespectful attitude at the time. But, life is always changing, and hopefully I can continue learning to change for the better.

This was only one of many "home calls" that taught me about "compassion" and "duty" and what it means to be a "doctor." Sadly, they don't teach these things today in medical school. But, maybe they should? It is definitely a character building experience.

## Religion and Churches in the Mountains

I have always known both my father and mother to be Christians, and our mountain heritage has deep roots in its family commitments, personal integrity (promises, and a man's word is his bond), hospitality and, sadly, stubbornness.

Religion has always played a large part in the life and culture of Appalachia. When you drive through the winding roads in the mountains, you will see many churches near the roadside that have names of denominations I never knew existed.

We also have snake-handling churches in the mountains of Eastern Kentucky. Not many, but some. These "snake-handling" churches are based on the passage in the Gospel of Mark that says "if they take up serpents and drink poison they will not be harmed."

"And these signs shall follow them that believe; In my name shall they cast out devils; they shall speak with new tongues; they shall take up serpents; and if they drink any deadly thing, it shall not hurt them; they shall lay hands on the sick, and they shall recover" (Mark 16:17-18, KJV).

Of course, this is not the typical Sunday morning service for most Christians, who believe this activity would be testing God.

Once, I took care of a patient who was bitten by a rattlesnake during his church service. He was an interesting patient and nearly died before I could get him up to the University for treatment.

He was bitten on the hand, and his entire hand and arm were swollen, black, and oozing serum. He had delayed several days before coming for medical care. But the most dangerous part was his blood count. Snake venom is toxic to platelets. Platelets are the part of the blood that produce blood clots and prevents us from bleeding to death.

We had given him all the blood products we had on hand, and his platelet count was still dangerously low. I was afraid he was going to bleed internally and die before we could get him to the University.

During the history and exam, I asked him…

"What happened?"

And he said, "Well Doc, I had been handling those snakes all morning with no problems, and then I started feeling 'proud' of myself, and decided to pick up another one. I knew I wasn't supposed to do that…and when I did, it struck me. It was my fault, because I knew better."

No question about it…handling snakes will challenge your faith!

I saw him again later, and he had survived but with the loss of some muscle function in his hand.

As a young boy growing up in Appalachia, I could not "see" or understand the things that God was doing to shape my life and future for His purposes. Some of these early experiences had a good influence on me and I have carried them with me throughout my life. Unfortunately, others did not have such a good influence and have caused me problems.

It is hard to summarize my childhood in the mountains of Appalachia and the effects it had on me. I shared some of these stories in the hope that it will help the reader to understand what influenced me and shaped my character, and which ultimately brought me to Russia. God has a plan for our lives, "if" we will only "listen and obey."

As I said, although I "hated" to go on "home calls" with my father, it had a huge impact on who I am today. It was the same with "church." I hated going to church. And, my parents forced me to go. I would sit in the back, write notes, and whisper to the other unfortunate children who were also forced to come to church. Even though I could write notes and whisper in church, the "Word of God" was heard by my ears, whether I liked it or not. I was **NOT** allowed to use earplugs in church!

*On one of our medical expeditions far beyond the Arctic Circle, I took this photo of a Nenets lady reading her Bible outside her home in the background. In this teepee we held a medical clinic to help her family. The temperature that day was about - 20 C.*

God doesn't make mistakes! Whether you are born in a teepee on the tundra of Northern Russia, a yurt in Siberia, or the mountains of Eastern Kentucky, God has a plan for your life.

"Your eyes have seen my unformed substance; and in Your book were all written the days that were ordained for me, when as yet there was not one of them" (Psalm 139:16, NASB).

If my parents were still living, they would tell you I was "stubborn and rebellious," and I would agree with them. But that same attitude is one of the things that has helped me to survive in Russia. I don't think I could have lived here for over 20 years and not had that stubborn streak in me.

If we ever meet, I hope and pray that you will NOT see that in me. But, it is there. It is one reason I can truthfully say, "I love Russia, and it feels like home… but it is a lot colder." We are always at "home" no matter where we are physically when God is in our heart. He is in my heart, and I love Him very much.

I have tried unsuccessfully to condense 40 plus years of life-shaping events into a few short pages. I am writing this book from Russia. But, how did I get here? What was it that brought me here? A large part of my journey here was because of my early childhood days in Eastern Kentucky, and the stubborn "faith" that I grew up with.

This background, I felt, was necessary to help the reader understand some of the answers to those questions. When I look back, I see God's hand at work from the very beginning of my life. I could have been born in NYC, Africa, Japan, and not have had a father for a doctor or parents that forced me to go to church. In which case, my life would be a very different story.

I had no choice where I would be born, or who my parents would be. My job is to Love the Lord with all my heart, soul, mind and spirit, and my neighbor as myself, and obey His commands. The results from that obedience belong to Him. All I ever did was say "yes" and show up for this job. God did the rest.

## The Importance of Promises
How do you feel when people break their promise to you?

I want to share with you how important "promises" are in our lives, especially if we are faithful to keep them. In the mountains of Appalachia where I was raised, a man's word was his bond. It was important, because whether you kept your word or not told the world about "you" and whether you could be trusted.

We all make promises. To our family. Our spouse. Our children, friends, and also to God. We usually know the people who can be depended upon to keep their promises, and the ones that can't. But the good news is God "*always*" keeps His promises.

"Not one of the good promises which the LORD had made to the house of Israel failed; all came to pass" (Joshua 21:45, NASB).

"Blessed be the LORD, that hath given rest unto his people Israel, according to all that he promised: there hath not failed one word of all his good promise, which he promised by the hand of Moses his servant" (1Kings 8:56, KJV).

I am so thankful that God always keeps His promises. He never fails.

When I arrived at the Russian border, the biggest question of my life was facing me. I had risked everything I loved, owned, and believed in to be standing here with all my earthly possessions in thirteen small boxes.

My biggest question was, *"Would God keep His promise to me?"*

He had promised me personally that "If I would obey Him, He would take care of me." The only way I would ever know if God would keep His promise was to have "faith" in Him and obey. I was about to step off the cliff into the unknown "Abyss of Faith" and receive the answer for that question.

CHAPTER FOUR

# how i knew it was God...
# and not pizza!

W e often hear Christians say, "God **called** me to..." A new church, Africa, India, China, to help the poor, feed the hungry, go here, do this, do that, etc.

But, what is this "calling"?

Maybe it was too much pizza?

How can we know when it is God speaking to us, and not some emotional experience, or something we ate? And, if we believe God is asking us to do something out of the ordinary, something that is illogical and not common sense, something that demands "faith," what should we do? How do we know it is God speaking to us, and not something I selfishly want to do?

These are very valid questions often asked by Christians, and they are difficult to answer, because there is no burning bush, lightning strike, or parting of the waters.

I am often asked, "How did God call you to Russia?"

"How did you know He wanted you to go there?"

I will try to explain what happened to me, and hopefully it will help others understand how God can work in their lives. But, my call or anyone else's calling is "specific" for that individual, and no one else. When God spoke to people in the Bible, it was usually "weird" and illogical. When they acted on it, they demonstrated "FAITH."

Universally, **we are all called to God Himself**, but we are not all called to do the same job. God has a special plan for each of us. He knows the hairs on our head (Luke 12:7) and even the very thoughts we think (Matthew 9:4). He has "called" us and planned our lives from before we were born (Psalm 139:16).

That is better than German engineering.

I cannot answer this question for others, but I can share a few events from my experience, which changed my life and helped me to understand God's calling for me. This cannot be *your* calling—only mine.

There are a few fundamental points that need to be understood before we embark on this journey.

First, it is important to understand that the "call" is between the individual and God, and only that individual is responsible for his call to God. The call of God is a private matter between the believer and God. As it was for the apostle, Paul.

"…When all this happened to me, I did not rush out to consult with anyone else…"(Gal 1:16, NLT).

Next: The "call" of God is to God Himself, and not to a place, a thing, or service. After we have accepted the call of God, He will then use us in His way, His time, and His place, as an instrument in His hands to bring Him Glory and Honor. Our "calling" to God is then seen through our "service" to others, in the place He "plants" us, and at the correct time in our lives. The call of God is mysterious, yet it is understood by the person being called. The issue that remains is one of simple obedience.

Next: It is God who will decide "how" and "when" and "where" to **use** us, after we "obey" the call. And, I should add the "call" is free will, you do not have to obey that call. But, if you choose not to answer the call, you will miss the most tremendous intimacy you can imagine with the Creator God Himself.

Oswald Chambers wrote:

> *God providentially weaves the threads of His call through our lives, and only we can distinguish them. It is the threading of God's voice directly to us over a certain concern, and it is useless to seek another person's opinion of it. Our dealings over the call of God should be kept exclusively between ourselves and Him.[3]*

It is amazing what God has given me over the years. I even have a real, genuine Mammoth Tusk from the tundra! Imagine the history and the people who have held those things in their hands!

Next: The "call" of God is for everyone.

> *The call of God is not just for a select few but for everyone. Whether I hear God's call or not depends on the condition of my ears, and exactly what I hear depends upon my spiritual attitude.[4]*

---

3    Taken from *My Utmost for His Highest (January 16)* by Oswald Chambers, edited by James Reimann, © 1992 by Oswald Chambers Publications Assn., Ltd., and used by permission of Discovery House Publishers, Grand Rapids MI 49501. All rights reserved.

4    Taken from *My Utmost for His Highest (January 14)* by Oswald Chambers, edited by James Reimann, © 1992 by Oswald Chambers Publications Assn., Ltd., and used by permission of Discovery House Publishers, Grand Rapids MI 49501. All rights reserved.

I found this most amazing book when I was working in Africa, called *My Utmost for His Highest* by Oswald Chambers. Although Oswald Chambers has been dead for many years, his teachings in this book have been my greatest mentor for many years. I read it every day along with the Bible, and sometimes more than once a day when searching for understanding on a particular subject.

The modern reconstruction of the English edited by James Reimann, I believe, is the best expression of his thoughts. In this book are many places where you can read about "The Call of God" and it will help you to better understand it. I highly recommend it.

Many of the ideas I am sharing are not mine, but his. I continue to be amazed at the spiritual insight and wisdom God gave this man.

I fear we have abused the phrase "The Call of God." It is often misunderstood.

Understanding these basic concepts above bring us to the last and most important point in understanding the "**call**" of God.

## WE are "the Will of God."

Often I hear Christians say, "If I knew what God's will was, then I would do it. Should I go to this place, or marry this person, or help this person, go here, or do this or that, etc.?"

Our lives are filled on a daily basis with opportunities to "do" the will of God. Jesus said in the Gospel of John (chapters 14-17), that He and the Father are one. He (Jesus) is "in" the Father, and the Father is "in" Him. When we are "in" Christ, we have accepted Christ as our Savior, and we have become ONE with Him, and ONE with God the Father. We could not be "one" with the Father, without first being "one" with Christ. So, in some mysterious spiritual way, through the Holy Spirit that lives in us, the three of us can become "one."

That is true "intimacy"—being "one" with our Heavenly Father and Creator of the Universe. Not even the closest marriage relationship has this kind of intimacy, filled with unfailing love and undeserved mercy.

"The will of God" is not difficult if we are one with Jesus and God, because everything we see, hear, touch, taste, smell, and feel is the same thing that God Himself would do.

When we are "one" with Jesus, we are one with God, and we have become the walking, talking, thinking, seeing, hearing, feeling, touching, tasting, smelling "**will of God.**"

**"WE"** become the "The Will of God" when we are one with Him in obedience to His call for our lives; and then we are "free" to do anything we want, knowing it will be pleasing to God. If we try to go somewhere, or do something that is against God's plan, we will know because of a resistance or "check" in our spirit. When the Holy Spirit shows us this error, we must stop at once and bring our lives back into a proper relationship with the Father; then once again, we are "free" to move in any direction we choose that is not in disobedience to His commands. Living our lives in obedience to God gives us tremendous "freedom," not a restrictive set of rules.

Decisions made freely in that context will never take us or send us anywhere, to do anything that God Himself would not do.

"If you abide in me, and my words abide in you, ask whatever you wish, and it will be done for you" (John 15:7, ESV).

I would like to share some of the amazing events and circumstances that happened personally to me during two years of fasting and praying as I struggled to understand God's call for my life.

## The Berlin Wall and Collapse of the USSR

I am a product of the 50s and 60s with all of the Cold War propaganda aimed at me by my government. I remember those black-and-yellow triangle radioactive signs posted on the walls of fallout shelters at schools and public buildings. I watched on TV the military tanks, missiles, and

Soviet soldiers marching through Red Square in Moscow, and I was told they were our enemy.

I remember seeing Premier Nikita Khrushchev banging his fist on the UN table and then take off his shoe and bang it on the table. The news reported that he said, "We will bury you." It was a tense time for everyone, even as a young boy I remember being afraid that nuclear war would come before I woke up, and the end of the world was coming soon.

But, as I was watching TV in 1989, I was amazed to see the Berlin wall coming down. I was now in my 40's and busy with my surgical practice. The sun was shining though my window, and I remember seeing the live images on the TV from Berlin, and noticing that it was nighttime in Germany.

People in Berlin were yelling and celebrating, and East German soldiers were poking their heads through parts of the broken down wall to see what was on the other side. Large cranes were removing pieces of the wall, and I was thinking…. WOW! I had prayed for this wall to come down, and now, here in front of my eyes, it was happening. Why are we "surprised" when God answers prayer?

This was in the news every day. Something new and different was happening in East Germany and Russia. You could "feel" it. I was glued to the TV as they arrested Mikhail Gorbachev, who was General Secretary of the Communist Party of the Soviet Union, and then a coup took place in Moscow. Tanks were rolling into Moscow, buses burning in the streets and grandmothers standing in front of the advancing tanks. Soon, we saw Boris Yeltsin climb upon a tank, the press took his picture, it was flashed around the world and the coup was defeated.

History was taking place right in front of my eyes, and shortly after that, by December 1991, the Soviet Union was gone! Disappeared! Dead! It no longer existed as a nation or country.

Chaos ensued and the country was in shambles. The life support system for a country of 150 million people had collapsed. The Soviet system had provided food, clothing, shelter, medicines, hospital care, ambulance services, fire services, and police services, and now it was in mass confusion. Everywhere, people were trying to just survive. Salaries were not being paid, but people went to work anyway in the "hope" that someday they would receive their salary.

On TV, I saw "bread lines" two blocks long of mostly elderly people standing in the freezing cold to buy "half" a loaf of bread. The news said that medicines and emergency services were in short supply, and they told many sad stories about the hardships people were facing. Gasoline was nearly impossible to find, and the ever present nuclear weapons which had threatened the west for so many years were now in danger of disappearing into the hands of the highest bidding terrorist.

Russian President Putin described the fall of the Soviet Union as the worst geo-political catastrophe of the 20th Century. I think I agree with him, because I have seen the suffering it caused so many innocent people. Russians, as well as people in other former Soviet States, sacrificed their sons and daughters to stop Nazism, and now they had lost their savings, dignity, country, and everything they had believed in. They had *faith* in the USSR.

As these events were unfolding before my eyes on TV, I was addicted to the latest news about Russia. At times, I could not sit down because I was so amazed at what was happening. I had to stand.

I saw the sad conditions of the people of Russia, and my eyes watered a bit at first, and later tears started to roll down my face. I thought, *Why am I crying? What is going on? I don't care anything about these people!*

In those days, I didn't know much about Russia except they wanted to "nuke" us. And, they were our enemy!

And everyone knows what you are supposed to do with your enemy…

But when I answered that thought, I understood immediately it was "the wrong answer"…

"But I say unto you, love your enemies, bless them that curse you, do good to them that hate you, and pray for them which despitefully use you, and persecute you" (Mat 5:44 KJV).

How could I do that? It sounded impossible! It was absurd and ridiculous!

I continued watching the news, unable to control the tears that would inevitably come.

But why?

I lived in a small Eastern Kentucky town of less than 2,000 people. I did not know any Russians. I had never met a Russian. My TV and newspapers seldom had anything good to say about Russia.

Sadly, all I knew about Russians was that a thick book named *War and Peace* was written by a Russian man and, of course, I had watched the famous Russian movie "Dr. Zhivago," but I knew almost nothing about Russia or Russian culture, and now I was crying because of their tragedy. It was the same for most Americans, and I was extremely ignorant about Russia. I did not even know about the famous Matryoshka nesting dolls.

The Iron Curtain worked! It had isolated a huge beautiful country and its people from the rest of the world. Sadly, my news about Russia was not always correct, as is the case today. The truth seems to have been sacrificed in the media for what is called "a good story."

Samantha Smith is known by nearly every Russian I have met. Most people in the West, including me, never heard her name or knew anything about her. But during the cold war she was encouraged by her mother to write a letter to the leaders in the Soviet Union asking why they wanted to make war all the time. In November 1982, she wrote General Secretary Yuri Andropov a letter after reading an article in *Time*.

She asked her mother, "If people are so afraid of him, why doesn't someone write a letter asking whether he wants to have a war or not?" Her mother replied, "Why don't you?" And she did. He answered her letter personally, and invited her to the Soviet Union and she came.

Many times during my travels around Russia, I have seen the name "Samantha Smith" on boats, and other places as a memorial to her visit. Sadly, I never knew this until I came to Russia. If it was reported in the news, I missed it.

I never knew anything about the tremendous sacrifice of the Soviet Union in WWII, or the tragic price they paid to live under Stalin's purges. To get some idea of this sacrifice and tragedy, "Enemy at the Gate" is a good film to watch.

Later, I learned of the Soviet sacrifice in WWII. They lost **26 million** people during WWII (the USA lost 418,500).[5] **That is 62 times as many people as the USA lost in the war.**

Each one of those lost lives was a personal tragedy; a father, a son, or even a mother or sister, who was personally known by God, no matter which country they fought for.

Now suddenly, after their enormous human sacrifice in WWII, and the terror of living under Stalin, they no longer had a country. It is hard for most people to understand not having a country. The exact number of people killed in Stalin's purges through execution and labor camps is unknown, but it was easily in the millions. It is amazing that this nation of people has even survived! Russians often tell me that Russia is cursed and destined to suffer. Even their authors wrote about it.

"Pain and suffering are always inevitable for a large intelligence and a deep heart. The really great men must, I think, have great sadness on earth."[6]

---

5    Website: http://en.wikipedia.org/wiki/World_War_II_Casualties.
6    Fyodor Dostoyevsky, *Crime and Punishment*, SMK Books, December 2009.

But, they were my enemy. Why should I care? I was very confused. I could not imagine anything I could do to help them.

As I watched these events take place on TV, somehow I seemed to feel their pain. And now, I was hurting, too.

I could not understand why I was concerned about the Russians, but it was clear to me that God was! "Why" or "how" I was involved in this was a *huge* mystery to me. But, I began to understand that somehow, unknown to me, "I" was a part of God's plan.

I started fasting and praying, trying to understand what was happening to me. Why was I crying? What was going on? What was God doing to me? And, most importantly…

Why me? I am a nobody, living in a small insignificant town in Appalachia. I had no political connections, missionary friends, or anyone who knew about Russia. Only God knew what was happening to me.

## Five Huge Impossible Problems

When I prayed, I began to understand that God wanted me to "go" to Russia. I didn't want to go! Why did I need to go? I never liked cold weather, and often wore a sweater in warm weather. Sometimes during summer, I would turn on the heat inside the house. I was cold natured, and I had no idea how I would survive there. How would it work? What would I do? Where would I live? Why am I even thinking about this? This is crazy.

I used to "joke" about being a missionary in the Caribbean. Lying on the beach under a palm tree, sipping coconut juice, and witnessing to the people who walked by. I think God must have laughed when I said that.

I continued to pray and fast. It took over two years to know that it really "was" God working in my life, and not some emotional experience or pizza I had eaten. Of course, I did not fast every day for two years, but I often fasted several days, and on occasion a week or more.

I remember kneeling and praying one morning, and saying to God that if He wanted me to "go" to Russia, then somehow my duties and obligations would need to be "solved." How that was going to happen, I could not imagine. It would be a miracle if it did! But, happen it did, and the events and answers unfolded very quickly.

I listed five things that had to be resolved before I could go to Russia.

My Children
My Family and Aging Parents
My Medical Practice
My Church
The Christian School I helped start

It is impossible to share all the miraculous ways that God provided an answer in each of these five areas. I never thought it would happen, but, with amazement, I watched as God quickly solved or provided an answer for each of these concerns, leaving me "free" to keep the promise I had made to Him when I was 14 years old.

## God's Promise to Me

One morning as I was praying about these issues, and in particular about my younger children who were my major concern, I believe God gave me His personal promise.

There was no trumpet blast, thunder or lightning, but as I was kneeling at my chair praying, this uninvited thought clearly came to me, and when I prayed about it, I realized it was true.

It said, *"If you will obey me, I will take care of your children."*

But, I knew God would never force my children to love Him or me, or to do anything against their will. God allows us to have "free will" and to choose whether we want to love Him or not. He will never force us.

But it was true. God could take better care of my children than I could. I could be the best father in the world, (and I was probably pretty close to the best), but there was no guarantee they would not grow up to be drug addicts, alcoholics, thieves, murderers, prostitutes or criminals. But God would be with them 24/7, to lead, guide, encourage and help them "if" they would let Him. I could not do that.

But I had to "obey" God for Him to keep His promise.

It became a matter of "faith" to believe this, and it was one of the hardest things I've ever done in my life; to leave the care of my two younger children to God and believe He would keep His promise.

This was a part of my early beginnings of walking in faith. I was able to understand a little of how Abraham felt when he was asked to sacrifice Isaac. Although I knew it was true, it seemed so illogical and against common sense. But faith is a "process" and we do not receive the full measure of it "instantly." It grows the more we use it.

"Those who come to me cannot be my disciples unless they love me more than they love father and mother, wife and children, brothers and sisters, and themselves as well" (Luke 14:26, GNB).

When God works in our lives, it is mostly through our circumstances. We see that He is faithful, and He keeps His promises. So, we learn to trust Him more…. and the relationship of faith between us becomes stronger and stronger, being built upon our love and obedience to God.

Soon, God started to do some amazing things…

## The Secret Trip to the Russian Consulate NYC

I am not sure, even after all these years, if my family ever knew I made this trip. I could not reveal my plans at that time. They would no doubt have thought I was "crazy," and maybe they would not have been far from the truth. But, if it was God leading then He would provide and guide my steps.

This happened while I was praying and receiving these signs and thoughts about giving my whole life to God. After all, if He had not saved me when I was 14 years old, I would not be alive to even think about it!

As I prayed and fasted, it looked more and more like God wanted me to "go" to Russia. But how? As I said earlier, I didn't know any Russians and knew nothing about their country. I was not an experienced international traveler and had never had a visa in my life, or knew what one was, or how to get one. All I knew was what I had read in the books. There was no internet in those days, so I depended upon what I could read in books.

After several miraculous events and numerous uninvited thoughts about keeping my promise to God to "go to Russia," I needed more information about this country. How to get there? How to get a visa? Where would I live when I got there? How would I get enough financial support to live there? I had a "lot" of questions that were unanswered, and I needed more information.

Somehow, I finally decided that I needed to go to New York City where the United Nations was located. It sounded like a crazy idea, and I knew nothing about NYC or the UN, although I'd been to NYC before. But I thought it would be a good place to start to get information about Russia. I have no logical explanation why I thought this was a good idea even after all these many years…but at that time it seemed like the right thing to do.

I had been to NYC before, when I was invited by NBC to be on the Today Show with Jane Pauley for an interview on my feelings about the current status of modern day medicine. That was easy… NBC did everything. They told me where to go, when to be there, and even had a limo pick me up from my hotel and bring me to the studio. I had also taken my children and wife there once for a weekend to help mend our broken marriage, but at the time I didn't know I was being manipulated by her "secret" lawyers for future divorce proceedings. They wanted me to buy a fur coat for my wife, take my family to a Broadway show, and entertain the family for a weekend in NYC. Her lawyers wanted me to do this so they could tell the courts I had a lot of money. The truth was, I didn't have the money, but like many men, I would do anything possible if it would save my family. I thought I was doing something good but it was a trap. It was sad the way I was manipulated, but maybe it was my own fault for failing to believe the obvious.

Nevertheless, I decided I needed to learn more about Russia and how to get there, so I "secretly" bought a plane ticket to NYC for the weekend. I don't remember what, if anything, I told my family, but no one knew where I was going or that I had left for the weekend. That was uncomfortable for me. In my family, we always kept each other informed about where we were at, and where we were going…even to the grocery store. I know that is silly for a lot of people, but I was raised this way so it seemed normal for me. My dad always knew where my mother was, and vice versa.

One day, I was in downtown Lexington with my father. Something came up and we needed to find my mother. There were no cell phones in those days. I was concerned about where she was and if we could find her, but my dad said without hesitation that he knew where to find her. He named a store, and we walked there, and sure enough, there she was. He said, "She always comes here." So, it was uncomfortable for me not to tell anyone where I was going. Somehow, I came up with something, and no one gave a second thought to the fact that I was not in town…I was in New York!

I flew to La Guardia Airport and rented a hotel room near the airport. I had no plans to rent a car because I didn't have the slightest idea how to drive in NYC, where to go, or how to get anywhere. My plan was to rent a taxi, reasoning that the taxi drivers who lived there knew where they were going. But after my experience, I'm not sure they do. There are so many foreigners in New York, and it seems many of them drive a taxi, and don't speak English very well. Where did all these taxi drivers come from?

On the way downtown, the cab driver warned me about trying to get a taxi during rush hour, from 3-5 p.m. and that it might be impossible, so I should try to leave the downtown area before that.

This idea to come to NYC was a disaster! I had no idea where to go to find anything, especially the Russian Embassy! Later I learned they do NOT have an Embassy in NYC, only a Consulate. The UN was also no help. Somehow, I ended up near Rockefeller Center, a place I remembered from before. I was very tired. I had walked and searched all day for information about the Russian Embassy and turned up nothing. Although I am not really stupid, at least according to my IQ test, I was not doing well on this day. I couldn't find "any" information that would help me get to Russia. I was feeling very silly, and my search seemed hopeless.

I remember being inside one of the large buildings downtown, I don't remember which one, when I saw a sign which read, "Information." And I thought, "Why not?" So, I went there and asked the man for information about the Russian Embassy. He pulled out at least 20 huge phone books and started looking through them for the Russian Embassy. This was when I found out that there was NO Russian Embassy in NYC, but only a Consulate.

Since I was not an experienced international traveler, I had no idea what the difference was between a Consulate and the Russian Embassy. All I knew was—it was Russian! And, I needed to find the place. It seemed like a good starting point!

I wrote down the address and phone number, and went immediately to a public phone to call the number… it was busy. I called again… busy. Again and again, it was busy! It was always busy!

Russians and people who have lived in Russia are probably laughing now because they know what is going on. But, I didn't. After living here for 20 years, we know it is very common for Russians to take the phone off the hook when they come to work. You don't need to answer the phone if you take it off the hook and lay it on the desk! This was very common in the early 90s.

Russia is very different from the western ways I am familiar with. I called many times and no one answered, and it was getting late. I thought, okay, I can call them when I get back to Kentucky. Little did I know that I could have called them until Jesus comes, and they would never answer that phone! It is the Russian way. How they put a man in space before the USA is a mystery to me! Luck, probably.

It was about 2:30 p.m. and my feet and legs were killing me. I had not eaten lunch, and no one was answering the phone at the Russian Consulate.

Feeling defeated and depressed, I decided I had to get back to the hotel so I could catch my flight on time. I walked out to the street in front of this big building and flagged down a taxi.

The driver asked me if I wanted to go by the "bridge" or the "tunnel." A very important question because of what would happen next. I said "bridge," having NO IDEA what that meant, other than I would be able to see something out the window.

I sat in the back, looking out the window at the buildings, and feeling depressed, tired, and berating myself for such a waste of time. Suddenly, I had one of those "uninvited thoughts" come into my head.

*"Why don't you stop at the Russian Consulate?"*

I sat up in my seat and looked out the window as we passed a street sign, and I quickly reached into my pocket to pull out the address I had written down for the Consulate. We were near the Russian Consulate!

I told the driver the exact address and asked him how far away it was… And he said, "Not far, just around the corner." Amazing!

I excitedly told him to go there, and in 3-4 minutes I was getting out of the cab in front of the Russian Consulate in New York!

I noticed a large number of police cars nearby, and my Cold War mentality kicked in to tell me it must have something to do with this Russian Consulate. Why all these police cars? As it turns out, it was a local police station.

Now what?

I had no appointment. I didn't know anyone, or what I should do next.

I prayed…

I stood outside a tall black iron fence with a huge locked gate looking at the sovereign symbol of the Russian Federation, a double headed eagle. All the things I had ever seen in the spy movies about Russia looked like they were true. This was a very foreboding and creepy looking place. More like something from "Transylvania." I was apprehensive and I admit a bit scared. No one knew where I was, and I had no idea what to do next, and all the Stalin horror stories and cold war images were passing through my brain like a rapid firing machine gun. None of the thoughts stopped long enough for me to even consider sorting out fact from fantasy.

Although the main gate was locked, there was a small opening where one person could pass though the fence. (There is always a hole somewhere in a fence in Russia). I went inside the compound and up to the front of the building. I was nervous because I was not sure if I was trespassing or not, but I needed information, and this was the closest to anything Russian I had ever been, so I went forward.

The windows in the front were all "glazed" over. They were one-way windows. "They" could see you… but you could not see "them."

Mmmmmm.

I looked around for a while, tried to open some doors, all of which were locked, and I could not see anyone anywhere. Was I supposed to "knock" on the door or what? All the signs and plaques I saw were written in some strange language with a few "Greek" letters that I recognized. I assumed it was Russian. I saw nothing in English. While I was trying to figure all this out, I noticed a button… Buttons are made to be pushed. I pushed it.

I heard a human voice talking to me in a strange language. I had no idea what it said or who it was. So, I did the airplane training thing and replied, "Say again please"… to which it replied "open the door" in English. I heard a large electro magnet click, and the door opened when I pushed on it. Not when I pulled on it! Backwards from what I was used to… but as you learn when you come to Russia… there are a lot of things that work backwards.

I was inside….

More one-way windows. Closed circuit TV cameras everywhere. But, no people. No reception. No guards. Nothing but a big black empty room. For sure it did not look friendly. I keep moving forward.

I finally see a "half way" window in the back of this huge dark lobby. There is a light on inside that room, but I can't see anyone in there. I walk over to the window and stand up on my tiptoes to look over the top. Inside, I see a Russian soldier sitting at a desk.

He spoke English in a thick Russian accent… (I assume it was Russian, but I had never heard the Russian language before, so I didn't know. It could have been Polish, or East German, but it was not Chinese.) Over the intercom, he said gruffly, "What do you want?"

Good question…. I wasn't sure myself.

I replied, "I want to talk to someone about setting up a medical clinic in Moscow."

Wow… that was cool. Where did that come from?

I didn't know what else to say, even though I had thought about what I would say when I finally found the place. It was the best answer

I could come up with at the moment, and as it turns out, it *was* the best answer.

I felt like I was stumbling around in a dark stairway late at night, with a few banana peels thrown in for fun, and I was feeling my way along the walls as best I could. Later, this would be reality for me in my ghetto apartment in Moscow during the winter months. I was afraid of what I didn't know. I was walking on unfamiliar ground and had no idea what the next step would be. I was anxious because everything was "unknown."

I see the same emotions in people who come to Russia for the first time. Everything is new to them, and their senses are flooded with new sensations of sights, smells, touch, taste, and sounds. It can be overwhelming for some people.

He replied, "Wait a minute."

I see him pick up the phone and talk to someone. I start thinking "What am I doing here?" "How did I get here?" This is stupid… and for sure it is not the typical "know it all surgeon" who is standing here. I didn't know what was going to happen next, and then I realized that "no one knew where I was"! They could lock the door, cut out my heart, liver and kidneys, sell my body parts for money, and no one would ever know what happened to me!

I remembered that in the movies Russians are good at killing people and making them disappear forever. The fact that no one knew where I was made me a bit uncomfortable, but then I remembered my Heavenly Father knew exactly where I was, and in fact had led me here, and I felt better.

After several minutes, I heard another one of those electro magnet locks buzz and the solider replies over the intercom, "Wait in that room." I walked over to the other side of the lobby, opened the door and went inside.

It was a large paneled room with a library that had only a handful of books on some large empty shelves. The few books that were there had fallen over on the shelf. Russian flags were everywhere, but unfortunately, they were not displayed nicely, and some were hanging crooked in their holders or ready to fall down. It was a sad commentary on a world superpower which had put the first man in space but was now crumbling.

I saw a couch on one side of the room and went over to sit down. I had dressed in a business suit and tie and not my usual jeans and pull over shirts. I looked professional, and that may have been important for the meeting that followed. I later found out that all Russian businessmen and bureaucrats dress in suits and ties for work in Moscow.

It was a huge room; there was no one there but me. I looked around the room and began to notice the closed circuit TV cameras there. You knew you were being watched. And then I saw the "hidden cameras." They were not too well hidden since I could spot them. The most obvious was in a small hole in the wall directly across from me. I noticed it easily when I saw a light reflection off the lens. The Russians who bugged the US Embassy in Moscow were more professional than this. If you don't know that story, buy me a cup of coffee someday and I will tell you.

I prayed…

I thought often about the fact that I had secretly come to New York and no one in my family knew where I was. I was anxious, but not afraid. Also, I didn't have a plan. Which is not at all like me. What to ask or talk about? What should I say to these people? "God told me to come here?"

Suddenly, the electro magnet buzzed, and the door opened. In walked a Russian Spy! I kid you not! I say that with a bit of humor, but if you have ever watched spy movies, this man was dressed exactly like one. He had on a raincoat, felt hat, and an umbrella in his hand when he walked in. Although it had been misting a little rain that day, I never expected to see a spy straight out of the movies come through that door. This was surreal! I felt like I was in the movies!

He removed his hat and coat and gave them to his assistant, and then walked over to greet me in English. When we shook hands, I noticed that he had a tattoo in the web part of his hand between the thumb and first finger. The same as many criminals I had seen in the ER in Kentucky. I shared with him my desire to start a medical clinic in Moscow and to do humanitarian Christian projects in Russia. He suggested that I come to Russia and "smell" out the climate. He asked me to send him a letter with my intentions, Curriculum Vitae, and any other documents I thought necessary, and then he "promised" to send them to people in Moscow that would help me. He gave me his business card; we shook hands and said good-bye. We had talked nearly an hour and I learned a lot about Russia from our meeting.

When I looked at his business card later, it turns out he was the First Secretary of the Permanent Mission to the United Nations for Russia. His fax and phone were on the card, which I still have it in my files today.

Later, after I was back in Kentucky, I sent him the letter and documents he asked for, but never heard anything more from him. Whether this meeting had any positive effect or simply left a thick file at the KGB about me is unknown. Still, the "uninvited thought" which came to me in the taxi at just the right moment on my way back to the hotel led me to the Russian Consulate, and it was another confirmation that I was in the center of God's will.

Thirteen months later, I was standing at the Russian border waiting to have my passport stamped and ready to enter the country.

## The Brochure Miracle

During those two years of fasting and praying, there were many events that happened to confirm God's call for me. I was seeking, praying, and fasting a lot, and I lost a lot of weight.

*This is me and my two youngest children with my niece. It is one of my favorite photos. Plus you can see how much the children and I loved each other. It was so sad to see our family destroyed. I had lost about 20 lbs in this photo from all the fasting.*

Often I wondered, *What is a medical missionary?*

I needed to understand what it meant to be a medical missionary. After all, I had never met one. I had no idea what their life was like, or if they ate snakes and spiders and wrestled crocodiles or what?

I needed to know this answer if I was going to understand what God wanted me to do.

But, I lived in a small town, and I only remember ONE missionary coming to our church in over 20 years. I never had the opportunity to meet missionaries, much less a medical missionary.

I continued to fast and pray….

In my medical practice, when the daily mail arrives it is separated into two stacks. One is "first class" and the other is "junk mail." This made it easier to deal with all the advertisements that come to a doctor.

My usual routine was to come to the office after surgery and hospital visits and sort through the mail. I usually started with the "junk mail" because it was easier to deal with, and besides, I didn't like opening the bills. So, I would take this pile of "junk mail" and look through it as I stood over the trash can. If there was something I wanted to read, I would put it aside to read later, otherwise, I threw it out.

On this particular day, I noticed a brochure about a medical missionary conference in Asheville, NC. This is not too far from where I lived and within easy driving distance. The brochure said that at the conference, you could meet "real" medical missionary doctors, talk with them, ask them questions, listen to lectures and stories about their work on the medical mission field. This was just what I needed and I was very interested in this. Then, I noticed the date, and remembered I had a conflict. So, disappointed, I sighed and threw it into the trash.

That evening after I went home, I could not get this brochure out of my mind. I could not eat. I could not watch TV. I could not read. It was constantly in my thoughts and would not go away. I understood God wanted me to go to this conference. Finally, I went into my bedroom and closed the door and knelt down to pray.

I prayed, "Lord, I understand that you want me to go to this conference and I am willing to go. But...I have a problem! I threw this brochure in the trash which has already been taken away. I could never find it again. I don't remember "who" is sponsoring the conference or "where" in Asheville it is located, or even the name of the conference. All I remember is that it takes place "somewhere" in Asheville, NC. But, I promise that tomorrow I will call the Better Business Bureau, Chamber of Commerce, Tourist Bureau, Mayor's office, etc, to find out where this conference is being held, and then I'll go."

Whew.... I felt better!

The next day, it was the same routine. Hospital visits, surgery, and go to the office. When I came to the office, I had "not forgotten" my promise to locate the conference. So, the first thing I did was to stop and tell my secretary that I needed to call the mayor's office in Asheville to find the information about this conference, and would she please get me the phone number.

Then I walked into my office, and here was my mail. Neatly separated into two stacks of "first class" and "junk mail."

***On the top of my first class mail, was another brochure, exactly like the one I threw away yesterday!***

I turned it over to see "whose" name was on the front to make sure it was mine. It was. I checked the address, it was also correct. I was amazed that this happened. Was it Coincidence? Maybe, but I doubt it.

So, in case you want to be scientific, what would be the probability of this happening? And, don't forget to include that it was the very top piece of mail! And, it was in the "first class" mail stack and not the "junk mail." It was clearly in the wrong place. Do you think there was some kind of message here? Was it a coincidence? I would love to have those odds in Las Vegas.

Oswald Chambers says that nothing happens to the Christian by accident…. I was beginning to learn how true this really was.

I immediately called the organization, canceled my conflict and made arrangements to go to the conference. When I talked with the lady about signing up for the conference, I "had" to ask her a question.

"Excuse me, but… I was wondering, how many brochures do you send out to each person? One or two?"

"One… Why?" she replied.

"Oh, I was just curious and thought I would ask…" I shook my head, smiled to myself and hung up the phone.

At the conference, I bought several books written by medical missionaries, talked with some of them, and I was surprised to learn that living in Eastern Kentucky was not a lot different than living in Africa! Only the snakes are bigger, they have to deal with malaria, and sometimes run away from "hippos." My first thought was, "Okay, I can do this."

After the conference, I read several of the books and began to think about going on a short term medical mission trip to fill in for some unlucky doctor who had been stuck in the jungle without a vacation for years. I would be able to experience what being a medical missionary was all about. Later I decided to do that as a "final exam" before committing to the new life that God was asking me to live.

Then, God did an amazing thing to show me He "really" is God…

## The "Burning Bush" at a Vineyard Conference

My brother told me about a new 'movement' among various Christian communities called "The Vineyard." I had never heard of it, but he said they were having some amazing miracles take place and were holding a conference in Cincinnati. He suggested that several of us go. I agreed, and so two married couples and I signed up. I was single at this time.

When it came time to go to the conference, my brother and his wife could not go, and the other couple also had a problem. That left only me. Since I had canceled my elective surgery and office schedules for this conference, it was too late to reschedule, so I decided to go by myself. I would be "alone" but, I could pray, read my Bible and seek God's will in complete solitude about becoming a medical missionary. Plus, I *really* needed to hear from God.

I had never been to a conference like this before. In the morning, we had lectures and sang praise songs. About mid-morning, we had a break and were given a sign-up sheet to choose "workshops" for that afternoon.

I read the list of choices which was rather extensive. I decided on a workshop and checked it, and…suddenly, somehow, I knew this was **NOT** the correct choice! Beats me how I knew that, but I did.

I sat down, looked at it again, prayed, and picked another choice. Again, I had to erase the checkmark. It was somehow also wrong. So, I prayed again about what to do, because this was getting to be a little "strange."

Then, my eyes came across a workshop that somehow, I KNEW was the correct choice. I cannot even remember what it was about, but the subject seemed unimportant and irrelevant to me. Anyway, I checked it, turned in my list, finished the morning worship program and went to lunch.

After lunch, we were supposed to attend the workshop we had chosen earlier in the day. I found the room which seated about 200-250 people, and I decided to sit about halfway back in the room on the left side. I was sitting in one of those large aisle rows that usually divides a large room in half. I had no seats immediately in front of me, and it gave me a good view of the podium and the room.

The teacher came and lectured for about 45 minutes on "something." I cannot remember anything he said, or what the subject was, *but I do remember what happened next!*

It is difficult to talk about this or write about it without quivers in my voice, and uncomfortable emotions that flood over me. Even now. This is so hard to talk about; I have seldom shared it with anybody. I had heard others talk about these kinds of things, but I had never seen it, or experienced it.

At the end of the talk, the man closed his Bible, and said, "I think God wants us to minister to some people who are here today, so let's pray."

We prayed, and he was silent for a few seconds, and then he said…

"If your name is Wilma, or Willie, or William, or Wanda, or something that sounds like this…would you please stand?"

Since my name is "William," I stood up along with four or five other people in the room. I did *not* feel comfortable doing so, but I did.

Then he said, "If you are not having problems with your finances or house payments, please sit down."

I sat back down with a great sigh of relief, because I didn't have any of those problems. My house had burned to the ground a few years earlier, and now I had no mortgage or house payments. I was paying rent. (See photos below.)

## Another Fire

There was another fire in my life, but this time I was not lying in it; I was looking at it. I was standing in front of my 110 year old house which had been remodeled and filled with antiques as it burned to the ground. Nothing was left. Thankfully, our children who had been at home at the time escaped without harm.

My wife and I had gone out with some friends near Christmas time to eat at a restaurant and have fellowship. While we were there, we received a phone call that our house was on fire.

We returned home to watch the final flames consume the house. Everything was lost except a few things that our brave neighbors were able to save. It is amazing how quickly everything you own can disappear in flames.

## Before the Fire

## After the Fire

The insurance company was able to find a way not to honor the replacement clause of our home insurance, and we temporarily moved into a small rental house. I had mistakenly believed that insurance companies wanted to help you during tragic times like this. After the fire, we didn't have much "stuff" so it was easy to move. But life and our marriage was never the same. There were difficulties in the marriage before the fire, but sadly, I never knew this until it was too late.

## Back to the Vineyard Conference

Next, the leader proceeded to "read their mail" as some people would say. He told those who remained standing "details" about their homes, finances, and mortgage problems, and gave them some advice, then asked them to sit down.

I was sitting there trying to figure out, "How did he do that!?"

Then he stood quietly on the stage, not moving, just standing there, almost like he was in a trance. The room was "uncomfortably quiet." NO…it was deathly silent! It was so quiet you literally could hear your heart beating, no one was moving. I was even afraid to take a deep breath and he continued standing there for what seemed like "forever."

Then he spoke, and I remember what he said!

I can never forget it…

In a quiet voice, that was somehow full of power…

he said…

"Would all the people who sat down earlier, please stand."

I hesitated…

Slowly…I got to my feet…

I was the *only* person standing!

From halfway across the room, I could see his eyes intently fixed on me, and he said…

"Your name is 'William'…isn't it…?"

How could he know my name?

"Yes…" I answered.

He paused for a second…

"Furthermore…you have a son and his name is also **_William_**…isn't that true?"

"Yes…" I replied.

Again, he paused…

"In fact, sir,…you have **_two_** **sons** who are named **_William_**… don't you?"

At this point, I am feeling extremely uncomfortable and very nervous, having no idea what he is going to reveal about me with his next breath.

I answered, in a quivering voice….and my insides were trembling like an earthquake.

"Yes sir, I do."

Then he said…

"You are here because you are seeking an answer about a special call God has given you… isn't that correct?"

"Yes sir," I answered.

Then he said,

"I have a message for you from God. God wants you to know that you can trust Him and you need not be afraid."

"You can sit down."

And the workshop was dismissed.

The meeting was finished, it was done—over—and I was left standing there with my mind filled with more questions than I could answer in a lifetime.

How did he do that?

How could he know my name?

Not only *my* name, but how could he know I had a son and his name? And how could he possibly know I had **two sons** whose names are both **_William_**? This is impossible!

*There are 4 "Williams" in my family. This is my father, me, and my youngest son who are all named William.*

*My dad and oldest son both named William.*

There was only one person at this conference who knew me, and I had only met him briefly, and he was not in this room. I am 100% sure he did not tell this man anything about me. This man had never seen me before. I had no nametag on. I never told anyone at this conference I had a son or sons who were named William, or even that "my" name is William. I registered as Bill and everyone calls me Bill, **not** William. There is NO WAY he could have known all this information about me, and certainly I did not share my deepest emotions about seeking God's will with anyone at this conference. No one knew this except God and me!

Was it a "burning bush" type of experience?

If so, what should I do?

Moses didn't want the job, and neither did I!

I have since learned that God seldom works in logical, common sense ways. You only need to read the Bible to understand that faith is not the same as common sense.

How could this man do that? He couldn't unless he had a deep relationship with the Father. Maybe this was why none of the other seminars I tried to select that day were correct for me?

Years later, I still cannot write about this without watery eyes, deep sighing, and a small trembling deep inside. I had just been introduced to the work of the Spirit of the Living God!

I was so shocked by what happened that my mind was spinning with questions trying to understand "how" did he do that? I left the conference room and went immediately to my room to be alone. I wanted to write down everything I could remember. I even ordered a cassette tape of the workshop so I would have the facts. I wanted to know this was real, and I had not somehow imagined it.

It is difficult to understand spiritual things if we use common sense. I heard other people talk about events like this, but I had never experienced anything like it before in my life.

Common sense and faith are antagonistic toward each other. If you can understand it, if it is logical, if you can touch it, examine it, stand on it, and it makes sense, then it takes no faith to obey or act on it. It is only when you are standing on the edge of the abyss, looking into the foggy mist of the unknown, believing that God will catch you if you jump, that you have the opportunity for faith. Only then is it possible to know if you have faith. If you jump, you have faith. There is no faith *until* you jump, because you are standing on the solid ground of logic and common sense, and that does not require any faith.

As it turns out, the cassette tape did not have the "ministry" part of the workshop on it. I was disappointed, because it would have proven what I just wrote. But, I suppose if I could prove it, then it would not take any faith for you to believe it. I would not blame you if you don't believe it. Faith is very personal. I have heard Christians talk about these kinds of things before, and I was always "skeptical"— until that day!

Faith becomes a possession of the individual only when it is acted upon. If you don't act on your faith, then your faith is dead (James 2:17).

You cannot have another person's faith. Only yours. Each of us must stand at the edge of the "abyss," and it makes no difference what religion or belief system you profess. Either you act on what you believe, or you don't.

God had just spoken to me in a very powerful way…. Now what?

*Even after I arrived in Russia, God continued doing miracles to confirm and reassure me that "yes" this was indeed His will for me… (and that I could stop worrying about it and get "going" with the work He had planned for me.)*

## Angels and "Probabilities"

I had been traveling in the far north of Russia for nearly two weeks. It was -30C most of the time, and on this particular night we were returning very late through the forest or Taiga. We were on our way home and all of us were very tired. We had traveled to some remote villages deep in the Taiga, doing medical clinics and sharing the Love of God. Many people cried, some accepted Christ, and many could not believe that God loved them enough to send someone to help them.

It was already very late and we had a long, cold, dark, drive ahead of us. The clinic had finished late in the evening, but thankfully, we were on the road home. It felt good to be "going home."

The sun had set about 3 p.m., and we were traveling through the Taiga on an old logging road. It was very dark. There was no moon, no stars, and the sky was gray and overcast. Yet, the forest was so black against the gray clouds, you could still see the road. It looked like a long white ribbon lying on top of a huge black blanket. We had already traveled about 4 hours and only met one or two vehicles on this deserted stretch of road. We were all tired and sleepy and had not seen anyone, a village, a car, or truck for the past 2 hours.

Suddenly…

BANG!

There was a loud noise that sounded like a gunshot. Someone had shot at us or something hit our bus. The motor revved loudly, and the driver pulled to the side of the road. Everyone was now wide awake.

The driver got out and raised the hood of our small bus to find that we were missing two fan belts. Not one, but *two!*

Now what? There were no exits along this imaginary interstate, no filling station, and no auto parts stores within a hundred miles. There was no place to find a fan belt in the middle of the night in this cold barren wilderness.

And, there were no cars on the road that could take us to the nearest place of safety!

Now that the engine was off, the temperature inside started dropping rapidly, and we began to put on all the clothes we had. I put on three sets of clothes, and could barely move. Still, I was getting cold.

One of the men walked back up the road and found both fan belts. One fan belt was intact, but the other one was broken and could not be repaired. The driver said without both fan belts we could not move. I suggested that we drive the bus as far as possible toward the next town, and when the motor froze, at least we would be closer to civilization and have a better chance of survival.

*Installing the one fan belt that was not broken.*

He was against this idea, because his boss had loaned him the bus, and it was his responsibility to take care of it. (*Even if he killed us all in the process*, I thought.)

I feared that we would all freeze to death, and they would only find frozen bodies the next day, or maybe next week.

Everyone on the bus was a believer, so we came together and started praying to ask God to help us with this situation.

The temperature inside the bus continued to drop, and now it was the same as outside. The windows were frosted over from the moisture in our breath, our faces and noses were cold, and we were slowly freezing to death, even though we had on several layers of clothing and big coats.

We continued to pray and move around, trying to stay warm as we sat there shivering in this huge deep freeze.

In Russia, the roads through the northern forest are usually a straight line. They log trees from here, and these old logging roads are the way trucks move timber to the mill. But there was no logging activity this time of year, and especially this time of night. We were on this deserted road… alone.

We had stopped near the top of a hill, and from my seat I could look off to the east for miles. There was nothing to see except a "gash" in the trees made by the road, and the foreboding dark forest on both sides. The road appeared like a tiny white ribbon slicing through a huge dark shadow for miles. No cars, no trucks, no towns, no lights, not even the moon was out. The closest point of civilization was at least several hours away, and walking that far in this cold would be deadly.

We continued to pray.

No ideas came to mind on how to fix the problem, and as I sat in my seat praying and looking out through the front window of the bus, I just stared into the endless darkness. All I could see was black everywhere and the small snow-covered road that trailed off to the distant horizon.

Suddenly, I thought I saw something. I looked again. Yes, it was a light, and it was getting bigger. It was on the road, and coming our way!

We prayed. What could this mean? If it was a small car, would they have enough room for all of us? It not, who would go to town and who would stay behind? Many questions were racing through my mind.

Soon, a large Russian truck pulled up beside us. The driver rolled down his window to ask what the problem was, and our bus driver explained it. Then I saw the truck driver bend over to get something from under his seat. He sat up then tossed a fan belt out the window that landed on the ground in front of our driver! And said…

*"Try this … I'm sure it will work."*

And, he drove away!

I couldn't believe he did that! He never stayed to see if it would work or if he could help us. He just threw the fan belt out the window, said it would work, and left. I thought it was strange that he didn't stay to make sure we would be okay.

But, will this fan belt fit?

Did you know that fan belts come in different lengths, different widths and different thicknesses?

So, what is the "probability" that this fan belt would be the exact **length**, **width**, and **thickness** that we needed for our vehicle?

Even though the driver's hands were nearly frozen, and I could see his fingers were blue, swollen, and they didn't move very well, he still managed to install the second fan belt.

It was really hard in this extreme cold.

He would only work for a few seconds before he would vigorously rub his hands together to make heat from friction and increase the circulation to his hands. After a few minutes he would put his hands under his arms inside his coat to warm them up, then take them out, work a few more seconds, and put them back in his coat.

He had pulled his coat sleeve over his hands as much as possible to grip the metal wrench through his coat sleeve. Touching bare metal at this temperature will give you frostbite.

After he installed the fan belt, the motor was so cold that it didn't want to start, but suddenly, it roared to life, and it was a welcome sound. Two hours later we were inside the city limits of town.

It was now about 5 a.m., the dark and cold still surrounded us, but it didn't seem to matter, because inside our vehicle the heater was working and we were warm.

So, what are the odds that on a deserted logging road in the middle of the Taiga of northern Russia, in the dead of a freezing cold winter night, with no cars or people on the road for hundreds of miles, that God would provide a fan belt for our vehicle that was…

the "correct length"…

the "correct width"…

and the "correct thickness"?

With God the odds are always 100% in your favor!

## The Final Exam

There were many things that happened to me over the course of two years, all constantly leading and pushing me towards the "Abyss of Faith" and "to do it God's way," not mine. The things I have written are only a few of the more dramatic miracles which God did. He did many other things, constantly reminding and reassuring me that He wanted me to "go" to Russia. But, I didn't want to go. Even after hearing God's confirmation at the Vineyard conference, I "had" to be sure. My faith was still too small to leave everything behind and "go" to Russia.

I am so thankful for the patience God had with me. I never saw a burning bush, there was no thunder, lightning, hail, or fire from heaven, but I believed it was His will for me to go to Russia.

But, there was still "one" final test…

It is not correct to say that I was "testing" God. I do not believe I ever did that. I was always sincerely seeking, looking, and trying to understand His will for me. I am sure He knew that, and once I knew His will then I would obey. I wanted to be sure it was not something "I" thought up. I was like Gideon, trying to be "sure" that it was God speaking, and not something I ate, or some emotional experience. Remember, Gideon was treading in a "wine" press when God called him.

I had promised God at the age of fourteen that I would "go and do anything He wanted, if He would not let me die." And, I planned to keep my promise, if it was His will for my life. I thought I was keeping this promise when I moved to Eastern Kentucky to practice surgery. But, as I look back, it was more my idea than His. Even so, the timing was not correct to go to Russia. There were no miracle brochures, prophecy, or miracles that I saw leading me to Eastern Kentucky. But, the calling to Russia was vastly different, and both God and I knew it.

The final test came in the spring of 1992. All these things and more were happening, and the pressure to obey God and go to Russia continued to build.... But, I was still unclear about "exactly" what it all meant. I had only a vague idea of what a medical missionary was. I had never met a medical missionary in my life.

It would be a huge decision to leave America and move to Russia. I would need to leave my home, my family, my medical practice, and everything I knew and was familiar with, to follow God wherever He sent me. Even if it was to the "Ends of the Earth." How would I do that? What did I need to do? What was the next step?

In the spring of that year, I received a brochure in my junk mail, inviting me to go to Africa and serve 4-6 weeks in order to allow a missionary doctor to have some time off.

By the way, there was only one brochure this time! So, I looked at my schedule and decided, "Okay, I can do this in May."

I called the organization and told them I was willing to go to replace a doctor if they still needed me.

I had determined the best time for me to go before I called their office. I told them the dates I was available, and the immediate reply was…

"There is *no way* we can process your paperwork so quickly."

I replied, "I'm sorry, but this is the only time in my schedule that will allow me to go."

"Where do you want to go?" she asked.

I said, "To the worst place you can think of, where no one else wants to go, or is afraid to go."

"Why?" she asked

I said, "Because that poor doctor probably needs a vacation worse than the others, and I am available to help him, plus, I am familiar with physical hardships and I'm not afraid to go there."

"Okay," she said.

And then she told me again it would be impossible to do this, but that she would talk with the rest of the staff, they would pray, and call me back next week.

She called back the next week to say…

*"I can't believe this. We will be able to process all your paperwork in time for you to go! Please get your passport immediately, and I will be sending you more information this week by mail."*

Isn't it interesting how when God is involved in our lives the pieces seem to come together?

They sent me to Kenya, Africa.

## The Secret Tape

When I arrived at the airport in Nairobi and collected my luggage, I was nervous, but at peace. On the plane, I cried huge tears that ran down my face for more than an hour. My seat partner was very concerned about me, and kept offering me tissues.

No one but me knew, that soon, it would be "finished." One way or another, it would be over and done with. I didn't know which way it would go, but I would know, and soon.

If it was God's plan for me to give up everything and trust in Him, then somehow He would reveal this to me, and I would know. If not, then I would return to the USA, and on the Monday after I returned I would operate on people who had been scheduled for elective surgery before I left.

After I stepped off the plane in Nairobi and collected my luggage, a *strange* feeling flooded over me. It is the same kind of feeling you get after being away from home for a long time. I had undeniable, indisputable, unquestionable...*peace*. I felt like, "I had come home!"

It was not peace like the world gives from lack of a war or conflict, but it was the peace "**of**" God. It was the peace of God *Himself*. They are different. "It is peace the world can't give and the world can't take away."

The organization sent me to a remote hospital in Kenya. So, I stayed overnight at a guesthouse in Nairobi. The next day a small airplane would fly me to the hospital. When we loaded my luggage and supplies, and added the passengers, I was very concerned that we were "overweight." Although I am only an instrument rated pilot, and not a "bush pilot," I am pretty sure we were overweight! Okay... let me say it bluntly. We were overweight! This is NOT a good thing on a hot day! And, yes, for my aviation friends... It was a LONG takeoff run, and I was not 100% sure we would clear the trees at the end of the runway...it was really close. We cleared the treetops by no more than 10 feet. There must have been some angels under our wings that day!

At the hospital I was given a room to live in, and I started doing surgery the next day. It was a challenge to go from the American operating room to one in the bush of Africa. Sometimes you have to be very creative and able to do most "everything." I did many operations I was never trained to do and gained invaluable experience. I never lost a patient. I worked night and day. I was physically exhausted at times, but felt wonderful inside. I knew, "I had come home." "I had found it." "This was where I was supposed to be."

And…

my life was about to change…

forever!

**The ABYSS…**

**It was time to step off the cliff and into the Abyss.**

**I needed to make a "long distance" phone call.**

The time had come. It was now or never. I was more than halfway through my program, halfway around the world and I was standing on the edge of a cliff, looking into this Abyss of "faith." I had to "just do it." After that phone call, there would be no turning back. No second chance. No way to undo what would happen.

Before I left the USA, I had "secretly" made a very detailed cassette tape with instructions to give away everything I owned. All my worldly possessions would go to my children, my family, and my church. My bank accounts, guns, pickup truck, grand piano, medical office, ultrasound, office equipment, everything, even my clothes. It would all be sold or given away. I was going to step off the solid ground of common sense, and into this unknown ABYSS of "faith."

I gave that tape to an attorney with instructions to give this to my sister "IF" I called him. I was about to make that call. After that he would take the necessary legal steps to close out my life and medical practice in the USA. I was never going back to what I was before.

My two youngest children had already been taken out of my life by a biased, unjust judge, and they lived in another city with their mother. Visitation would be scant, every other weekend for 48 hours and always at the discretion of my ex-wife. It was so sad. I never wanted a divorce or to be separated from my children. But our lives are often controlled by others, and we can't "fix" it or change it.

I had to travel all day to reach a phone, and make that call. It is not easy to make phone calls from remote parts of Africa. So, I calculated the time difference, and called.

The attorney answered, and we chatted for a few minutes, exchanged greetings, and then I said,

"I want you to give the tape to my sister."

He asked, "Are you sure?"

"Yes," I replied, "I have never been more sure of anything in my life."

"Okay, I'll do it," he said,

and then added…"I wish you the best of luck and I will pray for you."

It has now been more than 20 years since the lawyer gave that tape to my sister, and you can imagine how it felt for my family. It was like a death. We have talked about it often. It was really hard for my two youngest children because they were too immature to understand all the things that happened between their mother and me and the courts. As they grew older they have only heard one side of the story and probably never understood what happened between their parents, lawyers, and courts to cause such a disaster.

Divorce is such a selfish invention for everyone involved. The pain lingers for years in the hearts of people, especially children. I don't think the pain ever fully goes away.

Everyone thought I would be coming back from Africa and start my surgery as scheduled. But now, it was different. I was **not** coming back. The old "Bill" had died. He was gone. Sadly, he still raises his head once in a while and has to be dealt with (Gal 2:20). It was a very painful experience physically and emotionally. The only salvation in the event was the "peace" of God Himself which flooded my soul. I had lost everything else.

Over the years, I have tried to think if there could have been another way, or if I could have done it differently, but honestly, I can't think of a way I could have drawn a line in the sand and closed that door. In many ways, it was like a death for all of us, including me.

Needless to say, my family thought I was crazy, and they needed time to adjust. So did I. This was as new to me as it was for them.

## The Man Said, "My Wife Is Dying!"

It was a bright sunny day when one of the doctors at the hospital where I was working invited me to go with him to a remote African Village and do a medical clinic. He had a new 4X4 jeep that was in good working order, so we felt safe to travel some distance from the hospital. There were no cell phones in those days, nor did we have any satellite or shortwave radios.

We loaded the jeep with medicines and supplies and left the hospital compound. The compound has a fence with barbed wire since African villages are not always safe or friendly to foreigners. The current political situation was stable, but there had been some tribal conflicts in the past. Since many of the hospital staff were of one tribe or another, this would leave the hospital in a difficult situation if there was an uprising.

After we left the main road, we traveled on dirt trails that stretched across the African plains. The Great Rift Valley of Africa is an amazing structure, and if you follow it all the way north, you end up in Lebanon by passing through the Dead Sea and Jordan valley and finally into Lebanon.

We crossed a small stream (which would later become a raging torrent), and onto the plains. Not long after we crossed this stream, we saw a man half walking and half running across the plains. He began to wave as if in distress and started to run toward us. We drove to where he was and he told us that his wife was bleeding to death and he was going to seek help. She had just given birth to a child and the bleeding would not stop.

So, we invited him into our jeep and began to drive toward his house. After several minutes, we saw a small cow dung house with the typical African stick fence around it.

Imagine that you live on the African plains and you need to protect your family and livestock from lions and hyenas. One way of doing this is to build a fence by pushing sticks about the size of a broom or mop handle into the ground very close together. Then at night, the livestock and family are safe inside this small "fort" if the lions don't manage to climb over the top, which they often do.

*African Children in a house made from sticks before cow manure has been applied to it. The top part of their home already has the cow manure in place.*

The houses are formed from sticks, which are then covered with cow manure. The cow manure dries, and you have a dark stinky house, but I guess you get used to the smell. Interestingly, when it is dry it doesn't smell so bad, but when it rains, it does.

The village was made from these cow manure huts which were inside the fenced ring. There was a gate to the village, and we drove up near it and parked our jeep.

Inside this fenced ring is where the cattle, sheep and goats were brought at night and so the ground was covered in wet manure about 4-6 inches deep inside this fenced ring.

I remember very clearly a young boy about the age of 8 or 9 years old running toward us with a huge smile, and I could see his white teeth against his dark skin. We were probably the first white people he had ever seen. As he ran from the opposite side of the compound toward us at the open gate, you could see this wet cow manure "squirting" out from the sides of his feet with every step he took. I would have loved to have a video of that child running toward us, with that huge smile on his face, gleaming white teeth, and cow manure squirting out from under his feet with every step he took. It was an unforgettable sight.

We entered the compound, but stayed close to the edge of the fence where the ground was dry and you could walk without getting your shoes wet.

We entered the windowless house, and smoke immediately pierced our eyes and made them burn. There had been a fire burning in the center of the hut, but no chimney for the smoke to escape out the top of the house, so it followed the roof line and came out the door. The door was the only source of light in the dark hut, and it took several minutes for our eyes to adjust to both the darkness and the stinging smoke.

Wooden dishes lay soaking in dirty water in a nearby tub. There was no sink. The woman was lying on a leather bed made from cow skins, with some sort of sheet or fabric under her hips which was soaked in blood.

She had delivered a new baby a few hours ago. She was weak, moaning, with a rapid heart rate and low blood pressure. Her uterus was soft even after bi-manual massage and she continued to bleed. I began to wonder if she had a retained placenta part. If so, I had no operating room or instruments to do a D&C and remove it. So, with my gloves on, and under the best sterile conditions I could manage in this hut made from cow manure, I gave her a piece of leather to bite on, and with my hand I went up inside her womb and removed some remaining placenta parts. I massaged her uterus and the bleeding stopped. When I removed my gloved hand and my naked arm from her womb it was covered with her blood up to my elbow.

This is not something I wanted to see and would never do in a normal situation. I am so thankful that God protected me and her. I never had a problem with AIDS and she never suffered from any infection. Amazing!

Obviously, this cow manure hut is not the most sterile place to do a procedure like this, even if I had all the equipment I needed. But, God helped me to stop her bleeding, and save her life. Then we were able to pray and share the Gospel with the family.

After that, I always carried pitocin—a medicine that makes the uterus contract, stops bleeding, and induces labor—with me in my emergency bag.

She was stable, and so we gave her some antibiotics, vitamins and iron pills, and asked the husband to bring her to the hospital for follow-up or if she got worse.

Later I learned that she recovered without any further problems. Her husband was an unusually compassionate man in terms of African men. Not every husband was compassionate like him.

A wife is the property of her husband, and I remember one lady who was beaten rather severely by her husband but would not go to a safe house. Another time I had a female patient who had a large cancer on her leg and her only chance for survival was an amputation. The husband refused the operation. His reasoning was that as long as she had a leg she could work, but if we cut it off, she was of no use to him or the family. So, he refused to allow the amputation. She died and he married another woman.

This emergency caused us to run late for the village medical clinic and our return back to the hospital compound. It was nearly dark now as we returned to the small stream we had crossed earlier this morning.

About midday there was a large thunderstorm in the distance. When we returned to the stream we noticed that it was bigger and wider than when we had crossed it earlier in the day.

We took a "running go" and hit the water and started up the other side of the river bank… "THUMPpppp"… suddenly, I was almost thrown through the windshield by the sudden stop. Our jeep was now "high center" with 3 wheels completely off the ground. This was NOT good.

"High center" means that the axel of the vehicle was stuck on the ground and the wheels were not touching the ground. If the axel is on the ground and the wheels are hanging in a ditch then the wheels are left to spin in the air because they cannot touch the ground.

Plus we were about 10-15 feet from the edge of the river and the water was rising quickly toward our car. We got out of the jeep and started digging dirt from under the car to get the wheels back on the ground. We put dirt, sticks, and rocks into the ditches under the wheels so we could get some traction.

The river was rising "fast" behind us. That late afternoon thunderstorm had caused a flash flood, and we were about to be caught in it. We dug faster and harder. Sweat was rolling. It was now dark, and our hearts were pounding and our blood pressure was high. Suddenly we started to hear noises. Not more than 20-30 feet from our vehicle in the edge of the jungle, we could hear loud "stomping" noises. Some "big" animals were nearby and they were most likely hippos.

I remembered treating a young boy at the hospital that had been caught in the jaws of a hippo. It was not a pretty sight, and he would never fully recover or be able to walk normally. I didn't want that, so I worked with the door open, hoping I could jump inside if it were possible.

Thankfully, the 4x4 finally got enough traction on one of the wheels to pull us up onto more solid ground where all the wheels started to work, and we were out and on our way home.

Even traveling at night on African roads is not easy or a good idea. There are NO street lights, or city lights, and it is very dark. The people are also dark, and don't tend to wear white or light clothes that make them easy to see. You have to drive slowly.

In addition, road repairs are often not done, so a hole in the road may be huge, and all that you see are a few little rocks lying around the edge of it. So driving home at night was a challenge. But, God was good, and we arrived home safe and sound with the awesome opportunity to save a life and share the good news of the Gospel with many people.

I stayed at this remote hospital for about 7-8 months, doing surgery, learning about missions, missionary doctors, mobile medical clinics, how to share God's Love with strangers, and a lot more. I was at peace, and I had "joy" being available to go, and do "anything" God wanted me to. I was keeping the promise I had made when I was fourteen years old, and it felt good.

I told you one story about traveling across the plains of Africa, being stuck in the river while the water was rising and hippos stomping around in the bush. I could also talk about walking for miles to share the Gospel on Saturday (my only day off) in a remote African village, and to see crowds of people gathering around to listen to the Gospel. I saw medical cases with arrows sticking out of people in every anatomical place you can think of. I remember, in particular, one man who came to the clinic holding onto an arrow sticking out the side of his neck. Every time he went through a door he would turn sideways and hold onto that arrow. I even did brain surgery, orthopedic and urological surgery I was never trained for, but learned how to do it, and with mostly good results! It was an amazing time. God taught me a lot, and during my free time I was always trying to learn Russian.

I remember the first and most important phrase I ever learned in Russian. "Where is the toilet?" I thought that would be important to know.

Everyone thought it was strange that I was "not" going to be a missionary in Africa, and that God was sending me to Russia. But, my calling was to God, and my job was to "bloom" wherever God put me, and I was simply trying to do that.

When I arrived back in the USA, all my things had been sold or given away. I had no place to live, I had no bank account, and I didn't have a car to drive. My parents had a spare bedroom, and that became my new home until I moved to Russia. I had lots to talk about with them, but the cord had been cut and there was no turning back.

I started sharing my vision about going to Russia, and my brother told me about a medical mission organization that could possibly be my umbrella. People seem to think you are crazy if you are not working under a mission organization umbrella, but individuals were doing missions work long before we had mission organizations. I am not sure why it should be that way. The Apostle Paul would never have met the mission board requirements, and neither would I.

## Somalia Calling…But, I Thought You Were Going to Russia?

It was a beautiful warm summerlike day with low humidity and fresh air. I was in the process of raising financial support to go to Russia and driving along the beautiful Daniel Boone Parkway. I was on my way to meet with a mission organization that had expressed interest in being my umbrella coverage. The window was down, the radio was off, I was enjoying the fresh air coming in the window, and I was thanking

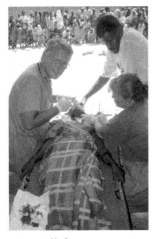

*Dr. Bill doing surgery in a doorway in Somalia*

God for such a beautiful day, when out of nowhere, this "uninvited thought" came to my mind,

"Why don't you go to Somalia?"

It caught me by surprise and I paused to think for a second, then I replied out loud…

"Okay, if that's what you want, Lord, I am available."

When I returned home after that meeting, I immediately called the organization I had gone to Africa with and told them I thought "God wanted me to go to Somalia," and if they needed me, or knew of another organization that did, I was available.

The lady promised to check on it and let me know. I didn't hear anything back from them, and so I thought, *Okay, it must have been something I ate*, and left it at that.

About 2-3 weeks later, I went to my dad's farm outside of town to shoot some clay pigeons, and do some "plinking" with a .22 cal rifle with my son. When I returned, my dad said, "A doctor from Samaritan's Purse has been trying to call you, and he wants you to call him back as soon as possible."

So, I called and talked with him, and he asked me if I could go to Somalia and help them for a few months.

I said…

"Okay, no problem. By the way, I called a couple of weeks ago to tell Becky that I thought God wanted me to go to Somalia. But I never heard anything back, so I had assumed you didn't need me. When do you want me to go?"

"Can you leave Monday?" he asked. (That was in 3 days!)

I thought for a second and realized there was "nothing" stopping me from going and doing anything God wanted!

So, we agreed, and I would pick up the tickets at the airport on my way out of the country. Wow…this medical missions stuff can be hectic at times.

Immediately, I went up to what is now "my old office," in order to gather some medicines and a few supplies. My secretary was still working there, but now with different doctors. We started talking and I told her I was headed to Somalia

*Dr. Bill treating a malnourished child in Somalia.*

on Monday. She replied, "What? I can't believe you are leaving again so soon."

I was in the back room looking in the drawers and cabinets to find some things I needed, when her sister came to the office and the girls started talking. I heard her say, "Pattie, can you believe it, Dr. Bill is going to Somalia on Monday." And, her sister started to cry.

The reason her sister was crying is that we found out that on the day I heard, "Why don't you go to Somalia?" she had seen the terrible conditions in Somalia on TV and had prayed… "God, why don't you send Dr. Bill, he is free and can go."

Why it took a few weeks for God to answer the prayer is a mystery to me, but it reminded me of the story in Daniel where it took 21 days for the angel to "break through" and get the message to Daniel after he had prayed. I wonder what it would look like if we could see the war taking place in the spiritual realm (Ephesians 6:12).

This time in my life was filled with spiritual events that I had never experienced before. The number of times God patiently worked with me to show me His will has not been repeated since. I have a close relationship with God, but the frequency and intensity of those special events are less. In the last 20 years, I have seen God do many amazing things, and some could even be called "miracles," but the greatest miracle has been the intimacy God has given me with Himself. There is nothing that compares with it.

I am writing this story from Russia, where God sent me more than 20 years ago. Why God choose that particular time in my life, I don't know.

One question I want to ask when I get to heaven is, "Father, why did you choose me? Wasn't there anyone else you could find who would do this job?"

So, I went to Somalia and served several months.

Here is an example of one of the newsletters I wrote when I was in Somalia:

March 3, 1993
Mogadishu, Somalia
Dearest Christian Friends & Family:
How can I begin to put the events of the past two days on paper so that both of us can understand? We had not been to North Mogadishu, across the infamous green line, since the fighting broke out last week. Even though we would have a military escort, the thought of sniper bullets from abandoned buildings was always present in our thoughts. The military too was somewhat more tense than I had previously noted. I suppose all of us were anxious—but we cannot do what God is calling us to do by staying in our house. We met for prayer—but today it was centered a lot more on protection. The people were noticeably less along the route today.

The markets were more quiet than last week. Everybody could feel the uneasy peace we had, even the Somalians.

Recent reports of the ambush and killing of humanitarian personnel and attacks on military convoys did little to make the 15 minute ride less anxious. The ravaged city—how could people destroy themselves, I wondered? This had been a rich country by African standards with museums, archives, national theater, a drama and arts center. All destroyed—all looted—even the roofs have been taken off—the windows and doors all removed—mile after mile of self-destruction.

What would our clinic be like today? We are the only medical team that has ventured across the green line. Today would be our second time at the "theater." The first time we saw a mixture of cultures and understood a little of what the "line" meant to Mogadishu. Yet, poverty and disease are not aware of this line. The clinic has been perceived by many here as a step in reuniting this city of war and hatred. Obviously, war lords who profit from devastating this country do not approve—hence our uneasiness.

We arrived in our military convoy to a scene that warmed my heart. Hands began to wave—children were shouting "A—merica," "A—merica" in broken English. People had heard we were coming back. Already, a long line had formed that stretched for over two city blocks. The Marines quickly set up their razor wire barricades and positioned soldiers at strategic points for our safety. We carried our tables, chairs, cots, and 8 footlockers of medications inside. We were ready!

I must confess that it "feels good" to be able to help people, particularly people in such desperate circumstances. In minutes, we were caring for the lame, the blind,-the deformed, many with crippling bullet wounds, all seeking help with their problems. It is so frustrating to have the skills to help people but circumstances prohibit it.

I remember once during the morning I was seeing an elderly lady who was totally blind in one eye, the other was partially blind, and she was crippled from arthritis. I looked up from this sad scene out across the theater, and there they were, the crippled, the diseased, the sick, and they hobbled across the floor to my Army cot. Each time I looked up, there they were—and they just kept coming, and coming, and coming. I thought about how Jesus must have felt as the crowds pressed in on Him, touching Him, begging Him to "touch me"…"help me." Yet, I knew medicine was only temporary. At most it would only help a few years, and Jesus was offering these people eternal life. I wanted to tell them, "Don't you understand, only Jesus can heal you? I can only give you medicine." In spite of the frustration, I also knew that these people would see Jesus today. In our smile, and in our soft touch, and in a kind word, and a gentle nod of the head. Yes, they would see and hear about Jesus in our actions. They know we are Americans and Christians.

As I was thinking about these things, I met Ruklyo, a beautiful 4 year old girl. Her smile immediately warmed my heart. Her body was small for her age, wracked with the evidence of war—malnutrition. Her arms and hands had been scratched until she had infected open sores with pus running everywhere. Why? Scabies was the medical problem—but I knew it was much deeper than that.

I heard the "mother" mention the word "orphan." My ears became attentive. I inquired further and found that before the war she had been "rich" in Burhakabo, but bandits had raided and looted their home. The father disappeared and the mother tried to manage the 6 children. Ruklyo has four sisters and one brother somewhere in Somalia. The lady with her thinks they may be in Merca but doesn't know for sure. The lady is not her mother. Ruklyo's mother died last month, probably from TB. It was several minutes before I moved on to the endless stream of sick, disabled people. I had to know about this girl. I suppose the inquiry was more for me than for her. My heart broke. I thought about my own situation and the difficulties it has brought. Yet I understood that "we" were lucky.

All my children still have both of their parents living and are, for the most part, healthy. Yes, Charlotte, it does get worse!

Next…later I see a lady I had seen before. She still has a tumor on her eyelid. Yet, somehow I must remove it today. I had wanted to last time but didn't have the time. Today…I will make the time! Maybe it will not be as "pretty" as if I could do it at home, but God has given me the skills and He has brought me to this place today. I must somehow make time!

Wow! What a morning—Did that man really have leprosy? I can't believe all the things I am seeing. More sick and hurting people.

I don't understand all of why I am here, but Father, I know You are here with me. It breaks my heart to see such disaster and sickness. But, with your hand around my heart, it gives me the reassurance that I am where You want me to be today.

My station is different than that of the others. I can look up and see the long line of people, their diseases are obvious even from so far away…and they keep coming, and coming, and coming, and coming!

Eventually, we had to stop, not because there were no more sick people but because…we were out of medicine. Today we saw 522 patients before noon. I am already tired, but now I must help the lady with her eye tumor. So we set up a makeshift operating room using a not so clean Army cot. We position it so the sunlight that shines through the hole in the roof will be our light. Actually, it was one of the best operating lights I have ever used. But, we did keep moving the cot and patient across the floor as the sun moved in the sky.

After the clinic, we visited the Somalia National Bank across the street from the theater. I found a blank checkbook and saw many canceled checks, deposit slips and things that had been destroyed just before the bank closed. We wandered around through the abandoned building. It was a beautiful place before the war, and I thought about all the people who used to work here. What were they like? Can I imagine what horror and grief these people have been through?

Back to the house, I am tired and would like to take a nap but not today—we must refill and restock 8 footlockers with medication and supplies.

## Beulalow Village

The Afgoi area again! Our first return to this area since all the unrest in Mogadishu and Valerie, the Irish Concern nurse was killed. Yesterday snipers were shooting at military vehicles along this road. Yes, we have a military escort. We are all tense during the ride and our eyes constantly watch for signs of danger.

We "set up" in a yard/barnyard combined. We put up tarpaulins to keep the sun off of our already scorched skin and head. Soon, the wind picks up and tears down the tarpaulins. We continue in the scorching sun. First, I notice 1 or 2 people are standing around my Army cot, watching me work. Soon, 15 or 20 people have crowded in, surrounding me. I finally ask the village elder to "give me some room." He begins yelling and waving a large stick and the people move back. It is so hot and dusty, I am thankful I have remembered to wear John's hat. We soon run out of medications again, and unfortunately, the sickest many times are so weak that they are seen last. The law of survival? The healthy usually push their way to the front and are seen first. We load up and start back to Mogadishu, alerted to the ever present bandits.

Dust burns our eyes, the sun is fiercely hot. My throat is dry and parched. The crops we see are devastated from the drought.

Somalia is a wasteland! Who would ever want to be king or president of such devastation? The "dirt devils" act up and scurry across the land. I reflect on the irony of the words devil, wasteland, devastation, poverty, sickness, disease. Herds of camels everywhere. People walking and donkey carts are seen *all* along the roads, but, where are they coming from and where are they going?

I can see for 10 miles but there are no houses or villages. As we ride along the dusty road, my mind recalls a small girl with seizures. She had been started on medication by me previously to control the seizures. According to her mother, she was much better. I asked the mother how she would get the medicines in the future. Her answer was that she has no place to get medicines except from us. I left "extra" medications and wondered if I had been any help at all. Was it worth it to come this far, risk my life, sit in the sun, heat and dust, for this? What would happen to this little girl after we left?

The important issues in life seem to be so intense here in Somalia. Then I remembered what Jesus said as He was talking about the hungry and thirsty, the stranger, the naked, the sick, the ones who were in prison. He said, "Assuredly, I say unto you, as much as you did it to one of the least of these my brethren, you did it to me."

Now I understand a little more why I am here. I prayed, "Father, I came because you asked me. These people are who you died for. They are precious to you, each and everyone. God of Glory, you came to earth and gave yourself to draw these people and us to you! What a marvelous God you are. I feel so small, so insignificant in light of what You have done. My unending servitude in the most miserable of circumstances can never repay you. Oh Father, I love you, but I am so exhausted, so tired, as I pour out myself for these people."

Then I was reminded about how exhausted Jesus was as He walked up to Golgatha—for me—for Somalia—and for everyone. Please pray for my strength, I am very depleted physically and mentally but I must continue as my Heavenly Father leads. For me, I cannot go back, I must keep pressing on—Philippians 3:13.

Agape,

Dr. Bill

After Somalia, I returned to the USA and started packing my things for Russia. You would laugh if I told you all the things I packed to go to Russia. I was going to a very cold country that I didn't know anything about, and I packed accordingly. Heavy coat, sleeping bag, metal dishes, can opener, etc… and a six month supply of peanut butter. I *hate* peanut butter… But that's a story for another day.

During this time, God graciously provided a church that paid for my airfare to Russia, and today, I still have the unused return ticket in my closet.

I am very thankful to that church for the support they gave me in the early years. Their monthly support lasted for 15 years and was critical to Agape and me in the early years. It allowed me to eat, stay in Russia, and do medical ministry. I am very grateful to their missions board and their pastor at that time, Wayne Smith, for their regular and dependable support. Wayne was a remarkable man, and I deeply respected him. I don't see how I could have survived in Russia without that support, and now I know that God will always provide if I am faithful. God had arranged a way to take care of me until Agape was more stable. He had promised that He would take care of me, and unlike people, God always keeps His promise! But, you will never know God can or will take care of you … until "**after**" you step off the cliff and into the Abyss.

When I first arrived in Russia, my support was about $500/month, and my rent for a ghetto apartment was $250/month. The refrigerator was at least 50 years old, and I had one enamel pot to cook in. I had lots of cockroaches for roommates, but they didn't eat much, and they didn't bother me at night. They stayed in the kitchen. It was really hard to live on $250 a month, but God always provided and I have lots of stories I could share about God's sometimes humorous provisions in the early years.

During the time I was in Africa, I always knew God wanted me to go to Russia, so I studied Russian and listened to the "Voice of Russia" on shortwave to prepare for my journey to a new land. Now I was here.

My income had dropped from six figures to what could be counted on your fingers and toes…. but, I kept my promise to God, and He had also made a promise to me.

*"If I would obey Him, He would take care of me."*

Did you notice how similar this was to what God kept saying to the Israelites and their kings?

"IF" you will obey me…I will bless you.

But, would God really keep **His** promise to me? Or, was it… just pizza?

CHAPTER FIVE

# brokenness

Pain...Sickness... Suffering... Sorrow...
Cancer...Death...Divorce...
Alone...Abuse...Betrayal...
Unfaithfulness...Rejection...Revenge...
Anger...Bitterness...Hate...

e tc. etc. etc. ... where does it stop?

*"We say that there ought to be no sorrow, but there is sorrow, and we have to accept and receive ourselves in its fires. If we try to evade sorrow, refusing to deal with it, we are foolish. Sorrow is one of the biggest facts in life, and there is no use in saying it should not be. Sin, sorrow, and suffering are, and it is not for us to say that God has made a mistake in allowing them."*[7]

---

7    Taken from *My Utmost for His Highest (June 25)* by Oswald Chambers, edited by James Reimann, © 1992 by Oswald Chambers Publications Assn., Ltd., and

I have been married and divorced twice and have four children. I have two children from each marriage. My oldest is a daughter, and my youngest is a daughter with two boys in the middle. I loved both my wives and was faithful to them. I believe that "vows" are sacred, and promises should be kept, but sadly vows and promises are not kept and marriages end in divorce about half the time.

It hurt me tremendously to see how my children suffered through both of these divorces. Divorce is so "selfish"—with little or no concern about others.

Young children are innocent in these events. Children are playful, and always asking questions about everything. They are full of joy, happiness, impatience, curiosity, love, trust, and all those innocent qualities that make them special. I especially enjoyed answering my children's questions about God and His creation. Everything from flowers to frogs was exciting for them.

I married my first wife at the age of 18, which made me a "young" father. I married my second wife near the end of my surgical residency when I was in my 30s. In some sense, I sort of "grew up" with my oldest children, and this produced some great "bonding" experiences that I remember with fondness and we still talk about today.

I had many special times with my children. We liked the same "toys" and learned to play new games together. We would climb up on the roof of the garage and look at the stars on a clear night. We once went to the appliance store to bring home old cardboard boxes from a washing machine. Then we cut windows and doors into the sides for a playhouse, and yes, I crawled inside and had tea. I also built a sandbox, and brought home a white rat from the medical school science lab in my coat pocket. (Imagine my daughter's surprise when she reached into the pocket!) Walking in the woods, teaching my children how to ride a bicycle (very tiring exercise for me), gun safety and how to shoot a gun, "real" tea parties at my home and once in Williamsburg VA. We made awesome blueberry pancakes, flew my private airplane to Canada for fishing, visited Yellowstone, and on the weekends visited the museums in Chicago. We flew kites, climbed mountains, explored Yellowstone, played together and watched God answer many prayers when we prayed together. I have many "special" memories of all my children during their childhood and I loved being their father.

No parent knows how children will respond to their parenting skills, what they will remember or ultimately how it will affect their lives. It would be nice if my children remembered all the good times with the same love and fondness I have. But, there is no guarantee how they will choose to remember those same events. Parents have no way of knowing in advance what their children will become as adults.

Children can grow up to be kind, sensitive individuals, or criminals, drug addicts, or even worse. We all know parents who did the right thing but their children didn't, and vice versa. God has given everyone, including our children, "free will" and everyone can "choose" what they want to do with their lives.

I know that the Spirit of God is working in the hearts and lives of my children, grandchildren and ex-wives. Divorced or not, they are "my" family, and I pray that God will work in their hearts to draw each one of them to His heart. But, whether they respond to His Love or not is their "free will choice."

Unfortunately, both marriages ended with broken vows, and it was a terrible heartache for me and the children. In my opinion nobody won, which is usually the case. Research shows that most families are worse off physically, emotionally, and financially 5 years after a divorce. It also shows that often a little time and counseling will save the marriage and make it better for the future years. But, people want relief from their painful emotions immediately and believe that divorce will give it to them. Sometimes it does, but most of the time those same problems are carried over into a new relationship, and the cycle repeats itself.

I really enjoyed being with my children, and my heart broke for them during those dark days. They were innocent bystanders with no choice in the decisions their parents were making.

I now live in a country of 3 million homeless children, by some estimates, and have had the chance to talk with many of them. They tell me stories that are so horrific and heartbreaking you would need to be "heartless" not to be touched by their lives. Abused physically, emotionally, and sexually. Neglected, abandoned, beaten, rejected, and unloved. No wonder they have such cold unemotional eyes. These are children whose parents should have loved them, but didn't. How it happens I don't understand, but in some ways it can be said that divorce also does this to children.

If you say to a Russian orphan, "Your Heavenly Father loves you," they cannot understand that. They never had a loving father or mother and have never seen or experienced what we call "sacrificial" love. Many divorced children have also never seen "sacrificial love" from their parents.

The orphan girls quickly learn that giving sex is a way to get the boys to be nice to them, but soon find out it doesn't last and is a poor substitute for the intimacy they so desperately crave, and it results in more depression, desperation, drugs and prostitution to survive.

Statistics show that 10% of the Russian orphan children commit suicide every year after being released from the orphanage; 80% of the girls go into prostitution and most of the boys wind up in prison. The outlook for a Russian orphan is not good. Institutions can never replace a home with a loving mother and father. Both are needed for a home filled with love and security, which children so desperately need.

It used to be thought that children who live through divorce would turn out okay after a few years. But research has proven this not to be true. Sadly, it seems that many children will always carry this burden inflicted upon them by their parents for most of their lives.

After following 100 children of divorce for 25 years, Judith Wallerstein wrote in her book, *The Unexpected Legacy of Divorce*:

"The people who suffer are the children. Contrary to what we have long thought, the major impact of divorce does not occur during childhood or adolescence. Rather, it rises in adulthood as serious romantic relationships move center stage. When it comes time to choose a life mate and build a new family, the effects of divorce crescendo."[8]

Her landmark study shows that her findings match the experience of millions of other children of divorce.

Near the end of my Surgical Residency I married my second wife. I was attending a wonderful church in the city where I was doing my surgical residency program. This is the same church I mentioned earlier where I reconfirmed my promise to God which I had made at the age of 14.

I believed she was a good Christian lady. She sang in the choir. We read the Bible together, we prayed together, we attended a Bible study together, and even talked about being missionaries together. And so we prayed and decided to make our vows before God and each other. I thought I had found the ideal Christian partner, and I believed that she also felt the same way.

But...

"Something happened." There is no other way I can explain it because I don't have any idea what happened. Even now it is an unsolvable mystery to me. I know that the breakdown of any marriage has two failing parties, and I am sure I failed in many ways. But in the beginning of the marriage, it would be hard to say that it was not as close to perfect as a marriage could be. But... "Something happened."

---

8    Judith Wallerstein, *The Unexpected Legacy of Divorce: A 25 Year Landmark Study*, Hyperian, September 2001.

We all make mistakes, and when we do we usually have two choices. One is to justify our actions and blame others. The other is to admit we are wrong and ask for forgiveness.

But, this mental juggling of our "justification" usually leads to bitterness, anger, and hate. Why? Because we are unable to think "I" did something wrong. Criminals in jail usually say, "I didn't do it," "it's not my fault," "I am not guilty," "I was falsely convicted." A few are wrongly condemned, but nearly all of them say they are not guilty.

Admitting our mistakes and asking forgiveness is the other option. It humbles and shames us to admit we are wrong, but forgiveness heals, reconciles, and brings peace. I am not "preaching." It is simply true. No one likes to say they did wrong, including me.

Forgiveness is always a better option, which is why God designed it in the first place. I need forgiveness every day. But in order to get it, I have to give it (Matthew 6: 14-15). And so, I often ask for forgiveness.

The divorce and child custody battle were physically, emotionally, and financially a nightmare for me. The divorce was like ripping my heart and soul apart as I was forced to separate from the people I loved. The only positive benefit that came from the divorce was to help me understand a little bit of how God feels when we reject Him and His Love.

An unjust judge awarded the children to my ex-wife against the advice of his own court appointed University Psychologist, and against the desires of our children. The children moved to a distant city, and visitation became difficult and reduced to 48 hours every other weekend—and at the discretion of my ex-wife.

Life is unfair, but we still must obey the law. It was an unspeakable disaster for me and my younger children. I was broken beyond words, the children were suffering, and it would never be the same again. There was nothing I could do to "fix it." I had tried everything and left no stone unturned.

Would I keep the promise I made to God at the age of 14? My life had forever changed through no choice of mine. Did I believe all the miraculous things God was doing to reveal His will for me? Or would I choose to believe all those events were against common sense, illogical, and that I had eaten too much pizza?

Faith and Common Sense are not the same. It is totally illogical for the Creator God of the Universe to send His Son to die for my sins instead of telling me to pay the price. Faith and logic are not, and cannot, be the same thing. When we are standing on the solid ground of logic and common sense, staring down into the "Abyss of Faith" because of something we "know" God wants us to do, that first step off the cliff and into the unknown is "faith."

As long as you stand on solid "logical" ground, you do *not* have faith. The greatest JOY you can know in this life is following Jesus, even if you step into the unknown Abyss. Because God will be with you.

God promises several times in the Gospel of John that we can be ONE with Him and Jesus through the Holy Spirit. Imagine, we can be "intimately one" with God, the Creator of the Universe. Jesus talked about this when He asked us "if" we wanted to be His disciple (Luke 14:26). Those relationships that Jesus mentioned are the closest we have on earth, but if we want to be ONE with Him and the Father, then there can be nothing or no one in between.

Jesus is not saying that those relationships are not important. They are. But, He is saying, if you want to be 100% mine, and a disciple over whom I can write the word "mine," then you must love me more than any of these. It is a hard teaching. Jesus is telling us that it is the most important relationship in our lives. Others, parents, wife, children, brothers, sisters, will come and go. Some will love you today, and leave you tomorrow. Jesus will never do that. He loves us with "unfailing love" and gives us "undeserved mercy," which we can't fully appreciate or understand without that "oneness" He wants us to have. We are "unprofitable and unworthy servants" even at our best (Luke 17: 9-10).

Being in the presence of God is the greatest thing we can ever imagine or experience, and for the faithful, He has promised us this for eternity. I feel like God smiles when He reaches out to catch the people who choose to make that step of faith into the unknown.

It is also important not to be "stupid" when exercising our faith. We should be obedient to the scriptures as well as the laws in the land, if they don't conflict with God's law. The way things are going morally in the USA, it may not be long before believers will have to choose. If it comes to that, then believers will have to choose who to obey, and they must be ready to accept the consequences for that action. I fear that many will fall away. God will not ask us to do something that is against scripture.

After two years of fasting and praying, and seeing many miraculous confirmations from God, I gave Him my broken life and chose to obey Him even if He took me to "The Ends of the Earth." And He did.

As a result, I left my medical practice, gave away everything I owned, finalized all the legal obligations for a new life, and stepped off the cliff and into the Hands of God.

Then I cried a million tears on the way to Russia. Dying is not easy. One of the scariest days of my life was standing at the border of Russia, waiting for them to stamp my passport and allow me to enter the country. Everything in my future was unknown. I had no idea what would happen in the next minute, or if there was anyone to meet me in this strange new land. But I knew deep down in my spirit, I was not alone, God was with me, and He was all I needed. That was 20 years ago.

"For it has been granted to you that for the sake of Christ you should not only believe in him but also suffer for his sake" (Philippians 1:29, ESV).

## Uninvited Thoughts

In this book I mentioned on several occasions how "uninvited thoughts" came to me. I want to try and explain what I mean by that. I am not a schizophrenic. In doing so, it may be confusing to many, probably not understood by unbelievers, and even confusing to believers. Still, I think I need to try to put this in words so that it will have some meaning, and hopefully some understanding.

When I say "uninvited," I don't mean that these thoughts were offensive, and I didn't want them to come. Only that they came out of nowhere, and I didn't ask for them to come, and I was not thinking about the issue when they appeared. You could think of it sort of like a friend you have not seen in years who knocks on your door and surprises you when you open it. They were uninvited when you opened the door, but you were glad to see them.

You may remember when I wrote about traveling down the highway, with the window rolled down, the radio off, on a beautiful fall day. I was not thinking about anything in particular other than the meeting I was traveling to in Indianapolis. From out of nowhere, without warning, this thought comes into my head. It was clear and fully developed. It did not come in pieces or in confusion, but clearly, all at one time. It said, "Why don't you go to Somalia?" It was a surprise to me. I was not expecting it, and I was not thinking about Somalia, nor had I been thinking about it. There was no reason for it to come into my head.

In fact, my thoughts at that moment were focused on going to Russia. And, there was no one in the car but me.

I didn't know "if" it was the Spirit of God speaking to me or something from outer space! I think we all have these thoughts, and the question becomes, *What should I do? So what?*

Obviously, we should not "obey" *every* thought. They must be tested. They should be prayed about in order to understand if they came from God. If so, then the question of obedience follows. It is important to remember, God will not ask us to do anything against His word.

"Beloved, do not believe every spirit, but test the spirits to see whether they are from God, for many false prophets have gone out into the world" (1 John 4:1, ESV).

After I returned home from the meeting, I had already prayed, and so the next thing was for me to call the organization that sent me to Africa and ask if they needed someone to go to Somalia. They promised to check and let me know. They never called back, and so I assumed I had misunderstood something. But, I was "available" if this was what God wanted me to do.

As I wrote earlier, about a month later I learned that this "thought" came to me at the same time that Judy's sister was praying. I did not know it was the exact same time I had received this "uninvited" thought until later.

So, how can we know when it is God speaking to us or if it is something else?

I don't have a formula or a decision algorithm to give you. I can tell you what Jesus said, and then you can discuss the rest of it with Him.

He told us to Ask, to Seek, and to Knock and it would be opened to us. He also told us that His sheep will recognize His voice. Our Shepherd will never ask us to do something wrong, but I am sure He **will** ask us to do things that feel uncomfortable and will increase our faith.

Hebrews 11:6 says it is impossible to please God without faith, and the disciples asked Jesus to help them increase their faith in Luke 17:5-10. In this section, Jesus talks about a mustard seed and an unprofitable servant. I believe that both were part of His explanation about faith, because in verse 11, it says, "and they continued on their way to Jerusalem." Faith involves the seed and the unprofitable servant. Both are required. But, "Why are the seed and faith so closely linked?" "What is the connection between a simple seed and faith?" They are connected, but that is a sermon for another day.

God wants us to have faith, as well as logic and common sense. But, faith and logic are not the same thing. They are very different and should not be confused. Still, faith when acted upon is as solid in the spiritual world, as logic is in the physical world (See Hebrews 11: 1-2, KJV).

I have never been more scared in my life than when I was standing at the Russian border with all my world possessions in thirteen small boxes, but at the same time believing that God had brought me to that point.

Another thing I have learned is that the more we obey His voice, the more we understand Him and how He speaks to us. As I have aged it is easier to know and understand His voice now than it was in my earlier years. The biggest problem I have now is "obedience"!

There are times when things happen that are not understandable even when looking back after many years. I remember once when I was preparing to break off the relationship with my second wife before we were married. We were not engaged, but it was clear to both of us we had a serious relationship. Then I found out that she was not being truthful to me in our relationship, I decided that it would be a good idea to end it before we got more deeply involved with each other.

So, I collected all those little things people give each other during their courtship, and laid them all out on a table so I could return them to her that night. When she came over, I told her I wanted to end the relationship and I explained why. Suddenly, one of those "uninvited thoughts" came to me which said, "How can you not forgive her after all I have forgiven you?" Good question! I knew I always needed God's forgiveness. I have never told her about this "uninvited thought."

So, I stopped, changed my mind and did not break off the relationship.

Years later as I look back at that, I wonder if I misunderstood. Because of that marriage, my children and I went through one the most horrible divorces you can imagine. It was so awful, it made the front page of one of the major state newspapers, and the pain and hurt is still there for my children and me. Did I misunderstand? Was it pizza?

I don't think so ... and here is why.

When I look back at all the pain and suffering that divorce caused, it is hard to see how anything good came from it. The only people who won were the lawyers. Yet, if I try to look at it from God's point of view, I see something different. But, my view is not clear because there was so much physical and emotional pain linked to the divorce.

Everyone has gone through "brokenness," if you haven't, you will. There is sickness, pain and suffering in all our lives, and this chapter is about brokenness.

People who know me will tell you I am different now and not the person I used to be. I agree. I am not saying I am better, only different. Even my counselor said it. All my life I was mostly an introvert; today, I am mostly an extrovert. Most of my life I was focused upon myself, today, I am focused on others and their needs even more than my own. I would probably give the shirt off my back to someone if they needed it. I am not the same as before I went through that horrible divorce. I see and feel things differently than before. I would never choose to do that willingly, nor would I want anyone else or even me to ever go through something so painful. But, life is not fair, and like a friend of mine often says, "I don't know how people can live in this world without God." I agree.

It is hard and painful for me to share these intimate thoughts with you, the reader. I don't like sharing my personal life, or putting it on display for all to see.

We like to crawl inside ourselves, and fold our arms over our chest, hoping to hide and protect our vulnerable heart. Or, we can choose to be like Jesus, open our arms and die to ourselves so that others can benefit by learning from our mistakes. Most likely, there are people who "understand" what I am saying, and I pray that my openness will help them to grow in their faith.

I believe the "uninvited" thoughts that came to me were filtered through the hand of God. All of them make sense, except the one that kept me from breaking up with my future wife. But even that looks correct, if I look at how it changed my life. Our lives are such a mess. Even on our best days, we are still the unprofitable and unworthy servants Jesus talked about in Luke 17:10.

Now, I have lived continually for more than 20 years in Russia. It is a new home for me much like Abraham had when he moved to a "far country." I didn't choose it. I don't know "why" God brought me here. But, God has not failed to keep His promise. He has always taken care of me. I have an amazing, intimate relationship with Him that is worth more than any fame, fortune, or power you could give me. I have peace and joy, and my God is always with me everywhere I go. The most important thing I have in this life is an amazing intimate relationship with the God of Creation, and I look forward to being in His presence forever. If I had not stepped off into "The Abyss of Faith," I would not have this amazing intimate relationship with Him that I have today.

Here is a true statement:

There is no greater "JOY" than following God, even if He leads you to the "Ends of the Earth."

I know...

I have been there... And returned to share this amazing journey with you.

Agape,

W. E. Becknell Jr. M.D.
(Yes, the "W" stands for William)

# epilogue

I kept my promise to God and have lived in Russia for more than 20 years.

What happened after I arrived in Russia and kept "my" promise to God? Was there any benefit in obeying God? Did it make any difference in people's lives? Did God keep His promise to me?

All these questions and more are addressed in the next book which describes the stories, adventures, miracles, struggles, pain, and loneliness of living in Russia for more than 20 years.

*Faith: Does it make any difference? If so, Why?*

I invite you to share my travels with Jesus and me across Russia to the some of the most remote places on Earth in my next book.

There is no greater JOY than following Jesus, even if He leads you to "The Ends of the Earth."

I know… I have been there! It is an amazing place!

# about the author

Dr. Bill Becknell was a successful Surgeon in Eastern Kentucky, living what he believed was the ideal Christian life with his wife and children when brokenness came and destroyed everything he loved. The one thing that survived, and became stronger, was his faith. He watched the Berlin wall fall and the Soviet empire crumble and after two years of praying and fasting, he decided to keep the promise he made to God at the age of fourteen as he lay dying.

He gave away all his worldly goods and arrived in Russia with his only remaining possessions—thirteen boxes and a promise that God would provide.

Keeping that promise to God was against all "logic" and "common sense," but he found that following Jesus to the "Ends of the Earth" produced something completely unexpected. "JOY"! He found "**JOY**" in the midst of some of the harshest physical, emotional, and spiritual circumstances imaginable.

He has written hundreds of newsletters, emails, blogs and comments from Russia and collected more than ten thousand amazing and beautiful photos during his travels to these remote and isolated places. He has traveled across Russia on every conceivable type of transportation possible from reindeer sleighs, horses, canoes, boats, broken cars, vans, jeeps, trucks, and buses, as well as on foot, sometimes without sleeping for days. And, he has lived with the indigenous people on the Tundra and the Taiga in order to share God's Love with them.

He has been interviewed on the NBC Today Show by Jane Pauley and by the Crossroads Canadian Christian TV network. He has had numerous radio, newspaper and journal interviews and has preached at many churches across the USA. Now for the first time, he shares his intimate, true life experiences in a book.

# how to order
# additional books

*Dr. "Bill" Becknell helps a Nenets (Eskimo) family*
*living in a teepee on the frozen Tundra.*

I hope you enjoyed my book, *Faith: The Abyss We All Face*. If so, I invite you to share this book with your friends and family, missions committee and other church groups. I will receive no profit from the book sales. All profit will be used for our ministry in Russia. To order additional copies of the book, refer to the contact information below.

This will allow Agape teams to "go" where no one else wants to go, "help" those no one cares about, and "share" God's Love with everyone, especially the people living in the most remote places on earth. Agape needs LABORERS and people who will support our ministry to the "forgotten" people of Russia. If you would like to know more about our expeditions and outreach programs or the Agape Farm and how you can "be involved," I'd love to hear from you. —W. E. Becknell Jr. M.D.

If you would like to invite Dr. Becknell to speak at your church or Missions Conference about our work in Russia, contact him at:

## Agape.DrBill@gmail.com

Agape Unlimited, Inc.
PO Box 50994
Midland TX 79710-0994
Phone (toll-free): 1-877-576-4504
Website: www.AgapeUnlimited.org
Email: info@AgapeUnlimited.org

# AMAZING "AGAPE" PHOTOS

This book features some of the finest color photographs in high resolution taken by Dr. Bill and Agape volunteers over the past 20 or more years while traveling to some of the most isolated and remote places on earth inhabited by human beings. This photo book makes a great gift!

**TO ORDER YOUR COPIES, CONTACT:**

**info@AgapeUnlimited.org or visit www.AgapeUnlimited.org/shop/**

*Cover photo on Amazing "Agape" Photos book—Tyvan Shepherd Girl*

Our prayer is that these beautiful pictures of remote people groups and places will encourage you to share the Love of God with those around you, or if God touches your heart, then to follow Him to the "Ends of the Earth."

You may also order individual photographs shown in the book for personal, church, and other non-commercial use. Contact us for more information.

Printed in the USA
CPSIA information can be obtained
at www.ICGtesting.com
JSHW082345140824
68134JS00020B/1900